**Oskar Wehr Reederei
Hamburg**

JÜRGEN WEHR (1)

OSKAR WEHR REEDEREI

HAMBURG

Von Gert Uwe Detlefsen

Fotonachweis:

Joachim Affeldt, Erkrath: 140 ur
Frank Behling, Kiel: 136 l
Cees de Bijl, Dordrecht: 87 und 89
Eilhart Buttkus, Hameln: 106 o, 116, 134 r
Gert Uwe Detlefsen, Bad Segeberg: 12, 17, 83, 103, 109 o, 130 ol, 135 l, 129 l
Sammlung Gert Uwe Detlefsen: 9, 128 ul
FotoFlite, Ashford: Vor- und Nachsatz, 54, 55, 67 ru, 68, 71 o, 80, 82, 86, 87 u, 97 o, 100 o, 130 ul + or, 133 o, 134 l, 138 ol, 139 l, 140 l, 140 or
Bernd Gell, Lübeck: 115, 139 ur
Jens Grabbe, Cuxhaven: 138 ur, 142
Eberhard W. Haase, Hamburg: 93
Hamburger Sparkasse: 104 r
Schiffsfotos Wolfgang Fuchs, Hamburg: 19, 22 u. 37 (H. Hamann)
Joachim Kaiser, Glückstadt: 15
Rudi Kleijn, Rozenburg: 129 l
J. Krayenbosch, Maasluis: 106 u, 107 o, 139 or, 135

Sammlung Stefan Lipsky, Flensburg: 10/11
Bent Mikkelsen, Ringkøbing: 132 r,
Marc Piché, Vercheres: 137 r
Olaf Schmidt, Singapur: 107 u
Atelier Sellschopp, Hamburg: 111, 113
Helmut Steen, Kiel: 138 ul
Peter Voß, Bremerhaven: 103 o, 138 or, 132 ur, 135 r
Klaus Peter Wilckens, Stade: 141
Lutz Woitas, Gifhorn: 109 u
Rasmus-Schiffsfoto: 95 o
Alle anderen: Familienarchiv Oskar Wehr bzw. Jürgen Wehr

Alle Risszeichnungen wurden von Alfred Schneider, Flensburg, angefertigt.
Der vordere Vorsatz zeigt HELGA WEHR (2) und der hintere HELGA WEHR (3).

© Verlag Gert Uwe Detlefsen, Bad Segeberg und Cuxhaven
23795 Bad Segeberg
Riihimäkistraße 38 a
Telefon 0 45 51 / 96 87 67
Telefax 0 45 51 / 96 87 69

Konzeption, Text und Gestaltung: Gert Uwe Detlefsen
Übersetzung ins Englische: Übersetzungsbüro Wesselhöft, Jork

Gesamtherstellung Satz & Druck Leupelt KG, 24941 Jarplund-Weding

Alle Rechte, auch die des auszugsweisen Nachdrucks
und der photomechanischen Wiedergabe, vorbehalten

All rights reserved. No part of this publication may be reproduced, stored in a retrieval system, or transmitted, in any form or by any means, electronic, mechanical, photocopying, recording, or otherwise, without the prior permission of Verlag Gert Uwe Detlefsen.

2. aktualisierte und erweiterte Auflage Juni 2001 für die Reederei Oskar Wehr KG (GmbH & Co.) Hamburg

ISBN-Nr. 3928473-15-8

HELGA WEHR (2) in der Kanalschleuse von Brunsbüttel.　　HELGA WEHR (2) in the Kiel Canal locks at Brunsbüttel.

In Koblenz geboren, aber die Rheinschiffahrt lockte nicht

Koblenz, von den Römern am *Confluentes*, dem Zusammenfluß von der Mosel in den Rhein als Kastell gegründet, ist immer eine Stadt der Schiffahrt gewesen. Von hier ließ sich der Verkehr auf der Mosel kontrollieren, in Koblenz begann, je nach Richtung, die schwierige Fahrt rheinaufwärts 'durch das Gebirge', oder die leichtere Fahrt zu Tal.

„Hier gab es viel mehr Wasser als an der Oste oder der Este, wo die traditionellen Küstenschiffer herstammten",

so Oskar Wehr, der am 12. Mai 1921 in Koblenz geboren wurde. Für ihn stand als Ziel die *See*fahrt immer fest. In der Familie gab es – wenn auch nur weitläufig verwandt – einen Admiral namens Oskar Wehr, der offenbar ebenso an dem künftigen Kurs des jungen Oskars mitwirkte wie der Reeder Robert Bornhofen, beide waren Rheinländer. Den Reeder Bornhofen kannte er zwar nicht, aber über dessen Schwester, mit der Oskars Mutter befreundet war, kam jedoch soviel an Informationen 'rüber', daß Neugier und Interesse an der Schiffahrt nachhaltig geweckt wurde. Die Rheinschiffahrt, damals geprägt von qualmenden Radschleppern und unzähligen Leichtern, hatte – zumindest für den jungen Oskar – jedoch nicht dasselbe Ansehen, wie die Seeschiffahrt. Für ihn kam nur der Beruf des *Seemannes*, nicht der eines Binnenschiffers in Frage. Im Dritten Reich gab es jedoch auch andere Karrieren, zum Beispiel in der Hitlerjugend. Oskar Wehr war ein tüchtiger und strebsamer Junge, gute Voraussetzungen für einen steilen Aufstieg in der Jugendorganisation des Führers. Bevor der allerdings richtig anfing,

The lure of the sea

Koblenz has always been a city of ships. It was founded by the Romans as a fortress at the confluence of the Rhine and Moselle Rivers (*confluentes*) and was a strategic point for keeping control over traffic on the River Moselle – where the hard upstream haul began 'through the mountains', or the easier downstream passage in the other direction. "There was a lot more water there than in the Oste or Este where the coastal shippers come from." This was how Oskar Wehr saw it. Born in Koblenz on 12th May 1921, he never wanted to do anything else but go to sea. This ambition was encouraged by a distant uncle – an admiral who also went by the name of Oskar Wehr. He and a shipowner named Robert Bornhofen, both from the Rhineland district, definitely influenced the course Oskar was to take as a young man. Oskar Wehr did not know Bornhofen personally but his mother was a friend of Bornhofen's sister, through whom enough information must have seeped through to arouse his curiosity and even permanent interest in seafaring. Paddle-steamers belching smoke and endless barges were typical for Rhine ships at the time but these did not hold the same attraction for Oskar as ocean-going ships. He was determined to go in for a seafaring career, not one as a bargee.

There were also other openings in the Third Reich – the Hitlerjugend, for instance. Oskar Wehr was a competent, go-ahead young man and so had the right qualifications for climbing the Hitler Youth ladder fast. How-

besuchte er mit einer Ausbildungsgruppe, die von der Hitlerjugend und der SS geleitet wurde, eine 'germanische' Hochzeit um Mitternacht im Walde sowie das KZ Oranienburg. Wehr: *„Dies beeindruckte mich stark negativ, zumal wir im KZ einer Bestrafung von zwei Häftlingen zusehen mußten. Die Häftlinge wurden zu 25 Stockschlägen verurteilt, und das Urteil wurde in unserer Gegenwart vollstreckt. Da ich mich verpflichtet hatte, konnte ich nicht so ohne weiteres kündigen."*

Seiner Mutter schrieb er noch aus Berlin: *„Ich trete aus der Kirche aus"*.

Seine Mutter – eine gläubige Katholikin – setzte Himmel und Hölle in Bewegung und machte von ihrem Vormundschaftsrecht Gebrauch.

„Mit Erfolg wurde ich dann im Juni 1937 feierlich aus dem Verein (der HJ) *verabschiedet. Außer der Arbeitsfront, für die eine Zwangsmitgliedschaft bestand und dem NS-Studentenbund 1942-43 gehörte ich keiner NS-Organisation mehr an. Nun konnte ich mit meiner Seefahrt starten, ich hatte die elterliche Einwilligung bekommen!"*

Das war 1937; endlich begann der Berufsweg in der Schiffahrt. Zur See wurde nun allerdings immer noch nicht gefahren, denn am Anfang einer seemännischen Laufbahn stand damals wie heute der Besuch einer Schiffsjungenschule. Drei Monate lernte er auf dem stationären Schulschiff ADMIRAL BROMMY in Bremen Deckschrubben, Knoten, Spleißen, die Bedeutung von Tonnen, Leuchtfeuern und anderen Seezeichen, sowie den 'Kompaß vorwärts und rückwärts in Viertelstrichen' aufsagen.

„Eine ordentliche Ausbildung", erinnert sich Oskar Wehr. Im Oktober 1937 hatte er die Anfangsausbildung beendet und kam an Bord eines Küstenschiffes. Das war die 120

Oskar Wehr

ever two events left lasting impressions on him. First, as a member of a training unit led by the Hitlerjugend and the SS, he witnessed a 'Germanic wedding ceremony' in a forest at midnight and secondly, when his training unit visited the concentration camp at Oranienburg. Wehr was left with a strongly negative impression, particularly as the unit was forced to look on while two of the inmates received punishment. Each had been sentenced to 25 strokes of the cane, which were administered in the boys' presence. *"I had committed myself to the course, so could not leave just like that."*

He wrote to his mother from Berlin: *"I intend leaving the church"*. As a religious Catholic, his mother did her utmost to stop the move, even to exerting her rights of guardianship. *"I was ceremoniously discharged from the Hit-*

Tonnen-Galeasse DORATHEA von der Oste, ausgestattet mit einem 80 PS-Jastram-Diesel. Eigner war Kapitän Hermann Hagenah aus Warstade, 'de mit den groten Holzschuh'.

„Nach vier Wochen wurde ich nicht mehr seekrank, der Schiffer löste seinen Matrosen durch seine bildhübsche Tochter ab. Wir fuhren Steine von Schwarzenhütten nach Hörnum, dort entstand ein großer Bootshafen. Wind und Wetter spielten keine Rolle, Kapitän Hagenah war ein mutiger und tüchtiger Kapitän, der weder Wind noch Wetter scheute. Auch wenn ich mich mit meiner ganzen Kraft in das Ruderrad legte, steuern konnte ich es nur, wenn ich etwas voraus hatte: eine Tonne, ein Hecklicht, ein Feuerschiff oder eine Landmarke. In Hörnum waren wir meistens am späten Nachmittag mit dem Löschen der Ladung fertig, und mein Schiffer lief dann unverzüglich aus. Bis zur ersten Leuchttonne steuerte er sein Schiff selbst, dann meldete er sich ab: 'Ick go mol eben ein beeten sloopen'. Beim Zoll in Cuxhaven weckte ich ihn dann, obwohl ich die DORATHEA auch bei Dunkelheit in die Oste steuern konnte. Aber auf der Oste steuerte der Schiffer sein Schiff meistens selbst, bis Schwarzenhütten gab es viele Windungen, Kurven und Engpässe. Die Erfahrungen der Steinfahrt von Hemmoor konnte ich bald nach dem Kriege gut gebrauchen, als ich zusammen mit vielen anderen kleinen Schiffen in der Kohlefahrt vom Ruhrgebiet nach Hemmoor tätig war. Törn Laden, Törn Löschen, immer mit Kohle. Törn Laden an der Zeche im Ruhrgebiet ging gut, aber in Hemmoor konnte immer nur ein Schiff zur Zeit löschen. Ich kam abends auf der Oste an, und alles lag da und wartete auf das Morgengrauen, um die letzte Wegstrecke zur Löschbrücke in Hemmoor zurückzulegen. Ich erinnerte mich dann an meine

ler Youth in June of 1937. Apart from compulsory membership in the labour movement (Arbeitsfront) and the NS Students' Organisation (1942-43) I never belonged to another Nazi organisation. So I was free to start in the seafaring profession. And even had my parents' permission to do so."

That was in 1937; Oskar Wehr was at last able to start his seafaring career. However he could not go to sea at once because, then as now, marine training college had to be attended first. So he spent three months on board the training ship ADMIRAL BROMMY in Bremen, scrubbing decks, tying knots, splicing rope, and learning about buoys, lighthouses and other nautical aids, and had "to memorize the points of the compass clockwise and counter-clockwise by quarters." Oskar Wehr remembers it as "good training." By October 1937 he had finished his basic training and was sent for service on a coaster, the 120-GRT galeass DORATHEA from the River Oste. She had an 80-HP Jastram diesel engine and was owned by Captain Hermann Hagenah from Warstade, known as 'the man with the large clogs.'

"After four weeks I stopped being sea-sick and the AB serving on board was relieved by the master's pretty daughter. We carried stones from Schwarzenhütten to Hörnum, where a large port was being built. Captain Hagenah was a daring, competent captain, who ignored both winds and bad weather. Even if I held on to the wheel with all my strength, I could only steer the ship when there was something ahead, like a buoy, a stern light, a light vessel or a landmark. Discharging in Hörnum was usually finished by late afternoon, and the skipper would always

Zeit von 1937 und fuhr durch und als die anderen morgens ankamen, war ich schon beim Löschen. Alles schimpfte, weil meine (spätere) ANNE unter dem Roof noch einen Laderaum hatte, der schwer zugänglich war und von Hand leer geschaufelt werden mußte – das kostete Zeit."

Im Dezember 1937 lag die DORATHEA eines Tages vor Wind auf Cuxhaven-Reede, draußen blies es mit zehn bis elf aus Nordwest.

"Ich mußte Grünkohl kochen, so nebenbei. Ich kannte weder Grünkohl noch konnte ich kochen. Kapitän Ehlers mit der Tjalk KEHRWIEDER lag längsseite. >Na Moses, wat gifft dat denn hüt to eeten?< Grünkohl!"

>Kannste den auch richtig machen?< Oskar hatte keine Ahnung, sein Schiffer war beim Schiffshändler an Land. Ehlers: 'Jung, dor must du'n beten Gasöl ranmoken, nich so veel, een Fingerhut full'.

Natürlich hörte der Moses auf den Ratschlag des erfahrenen Kapitäns. Dann 12 Uhr, Mittagessen. 'Hest di Petroleumlamp nich sauber!' war der erste Ausstoß, aber dann kam es dicke. Vorsorglich nahm Oskar Reißaus und stürzte auf die KEHRWIEDER:

"Kapitän Ehlers, nun machen Sie Ihren Scherz mal wieder gut!"

Er bekam Streit mit dem zornigen Kapitän Hagenah, Schiffsjunge Oskar zog sich zurück.

"Nachdem wir auf ein Stack gelaufen waren und ein Leck hatten, das wir mit einer Speckseite abgedichtet hatten, kamen wir Weihnachten bis Geversdorf an der Oste. Dichtes Treibeis verhinderte die Weiterfahrt. Der Kapitän und seine Tochter kamen mit dem Beiboot eben noch an Land. Ich saß an Bord und hatte nichts zu essen. Am 1. Weihnachtstag passierte nicht viel, ich trieb mit dem Schiff im Eis und mit den

Eine Galeasse auf der Elbe.
A galeass on the river Elbe.

sail at once. He would steer the ship until we reached the first buoy, then he would turn in 'to have forty winks.' When we reached Cuxhaven Customs I would wake him again, even though by then I was able to steer the DORATHEA into the Oste after dark. But the skipper preferred to steer the ship there himself, as the river meanders through numerous bends and narrow stretches before reaching Schwarzenhütten."

"The experience in carrying stones from Hemmoor stood me in good stead after the war when, with many other small vessels, I joined the coal trade between the Ruhr area and Hemmoor. Loading, discharging... and nothing but coal. Loading at the pit in the Ruhr was fairly easy, but only one ship could be discharged at a time in Hemmoor. We arrived

Küstensegler auf der Unterelbe   Coastal sailships on the lower Elbe.

in the Oste in the evening and all the ships there were waiting for dawn and the last leg of the trip, so they could discharge at the pier at Hemmoor. It reminded me of how I had spent 1937, so I didn't stop – just sailed on. By the time the others arrived the next morning, my ship was already discharging. Everyone was swearing, because the hold extended below the 'roof' of (what later became) the ANNE. Access to it was hard, so cargo had to be shovelled out by hand – and that took time."
Once, in December 1937, the DORATHEA was lying on the roads off Cuxhaven with a north-westerly gale of force ten to eleven blowing out at sea. "Apart from all the other things I had to do, I had to cook green cabbage . I'd never heard of green cabbage and I couldn't even cook. Lying alongside us was Captain Ehlers with his tjalk, the KEHRWIEDER. 'What are you having for lunch today, son?' 'Green Cabbage,' I replied, and he asked whether I knew how to cook it right. 'Just add a drop of gas oil, lad – not too much, just a thimble-full.' *Of course the young lad followed the experienced Captain's advice. Come noon, it was time for lunch.* 'Didn't you clean the petroleum lamp?' *The first expletive was followed by worse. Oskar fled, taking refuge aboard the KEHRWIEDER.* 'Captain Ehlers – time we made up for the bad joke.' *Captain Hagenah fumed while Oskar had vanished.*
"We ran into a breakwater and sealed the leak with a side of bacon. On Christmas Eve we reached Geversdorf on the River Oste. Thick ice stopped us going further. The skipper and his daughter just managed to get ashore in the dinghy. I was left on board with nothing to eat. Nothing much happened on Christmas Day, I drifted up and down with the tide and

Gezeiten so auf und ab. Am zweiten Weihnachtstag kam Geschrei von Land. Kapitän, Zoll und ein Mann von der Werft gaben mir per Grölen Anweisungen. Der Zoll erlaubte das Lösen der Plombe, damit ich aus dem Zollspind etwas zu Essen bekam. Der Kapitän erklärte mir das Entwässern der Maschine. So doof war ich nicht, denn den starken Frost hatte ich schon deshalb gemerkt, weil ich in der Koje anfror, und darum hatte ich die Maschine des öfteren warmlaufen lassen. Der Werftmann kümmerte sich per Geschrei um unsere Leckage. Alle Probleme lösten sich etwa acht Tage später, als unser Kapitän an Bord kam (mit einem Weihnachtspaket von meiner Mutter). Nun konnten wir auf der Geversdorfer Werft aufslippen, um unser Leck richtig abzudichten."

the ice. On Boxing Day I heard a lot of noise from ashore, where the Captain, a Customs officer and a man from the shipyard were yelling instructions. The man from the Customs let me open the bonded stores to get something to eat and the skipper explained how to drain water off the engine. I wasn't that stupid – I knew we'd had severe frost as I'd frozen in my bunk, so I had warmed the engine up several times during the night to stay warm. The man from the shipyard kept shouting about the leak. About a week later all our problems were solved, when the Captain came back on board (with a Christmas parcel for me from my mother). It was time to haul the ship up the slip and have the leak repaired properly."

Der Bugspriet eines Küstenseglers. *Bowsprit of a coastal sailship.*

Auf kleinen Schiffen wurde viel gelernt

Bei Hermann Hagenah lernte Oskar Wehr die Seefahrt richtig kennen. Was es zu Essen gab, 'war zwar fast immer mau'. Der Schiffstochter machte Moses Oskar oft Vorwürfe, ihr Vater sei ein Ausbeuter, weil er auf Segeltuch schlafen müsse:

„Meine Koje war an Deck im Roof, wo gleichzeitig auch gekocht wurde. Leider war der Aufbau so rott, daß die See von Backbord nach Steuerbord durch das Roof lief – je nach Seegang wurde meine Koje naß oder blieb trokken!" Die Kapitänstochter Thea ging mit Wache und faßte auch schon mal das Ruder an, wenn die Maschine abgeschmiert werden mußte, oder sie hielt sich für alle Fälle bereit. Kapitän Hagenah war allerdings sehr sparsam, zum Waschen der weißen Farbe gab es nur ganz feinen Seesand, für Caustic Soda gab er kein Geld aus, und alte Segeltuchlappen. Den Vorwurf des Geizes konterte die junge Damen immer mit einem schnippischen 'mein Vater hat A 5', weil die meisten anderen Küstenschiffer nur ein kleines Patent besaßen. Jedenfalls lernte Oskar viel, vor allem die Selbständigkeit. Sein Schiffer ließ ihn in Schwarzenhütten das Schiff mit dem Strom bzw. der Flut umdrehen, ein Vorgang, der Fingerspitzengefühl und Umsicht erforderte. Dabei half ihm anfangs Fährmann Julius – gegen einen kleinen Obolus z. B. in Form eines Paketes Tabaks. Dann lernte Oskar Wehr einen Matrosen kennen, der ihm etwas von der BRIGITTE RAABE erzählte. Er wurde neugierig und der Matrose berichtete, daß die mit 375 BRT vermessene, 1920 im norwegischen Arendal gebaute Schonerbark 'überall'

An education on small ships

Oskar Wehr learned a lot about shipping on Herman Hagenah's ships. On the whole, food on board was 'mediocre'. Oskar complained to the skipper's daughter that her father exploited him because he made him sleep on canvas: *"My bunk was in the 'roof' - on deck – where the galley was. The superstructure had rotted away so badly that seawater ran through it from port to starboard. Depending on the seas, my bunk would be soaked or stay dry."* The skipper's daughter, Thea, went on bridge watch and would even take the wheel when the engine needed greasing – or she just helped when she was needed. Captain Hagenah kept a tight budget. Only very fine sand was used to clean the white paint. He refused to spend money on caustic soda or sail cloth. To accusations that he was tight-fisted, the young lady would reply 'but my father has a master's license.' Most skippers on coastal vessels were not so well qualified. At least Oskar Wehr learned to be independent. At Schwarzenhütten the skipper let him turn the ship with the incoming or outgoing tide, which required a fair amount of care and feeling. At first he was helped by the ferryman, Julius, for a small consideration, such as a packet of tobacco. Then Oskar met a seaman who told him about the BRIGITTE RAABE. This aroused his curiosity. The sailor told him that the schooner was 375 GRT and had been built in Arendal, in Norway, in 1920. The ship 'sailed everywhere' – to all ports. The only trouble was one had to pay one's way. To which Wehr replied: *"I haven't got any money*

hinfuhr, kein Hafen sei ihr weit genug. Allerdings müßte man dazubezahlen. Wehr daraufhin, „*Geld habe ich ja nicht, denn würde ich ja auf einem Schulschiff fahren!*".

Er schrieb jedoch an den Rostocker Eigner Fritz Raabe, ob er denn nicht als (nichtbezahlte) Stammbesatzung fahren könnte. Das konnte er, und so wurde er Mitglied der elfköpfigen Stammbesatzung. Zur Betreuung des 125-PS-Skandia-Motors hatte sich der Eigner sogar einen Maschinisten gegönnt. Oskar bekam den Posten des Zimmermanns und lernte Kalfatern, das Bedienen des Ankerspills und vieles mehr. Bei schlechtem Wetter mußte der Moses den Decksmotor bedienen, der über eine Kapillarkette die Pumpen an Deck betrieb. Das kam häufig vor, da das Holzschiff 'leckte wie ein Sieb'. Die Lenzpumpen standen an Deck und mußten in der Regel morgens, mittags und abends mit der Hand bedient werden. Nur wenn wegen überkommenden Wassers – was auf See schnell passierte – der Handbetrieb nicht mehr gegenan kam, durften der Moses den Motor zur Hilfe nehmen. Die Verpflegung war dürftig:

„*Morgens ein oder zwei Teller Milchsuppe – mit oder ohne Brot –, mittags irgendwas, und manchmal hatten wir abends auch noch Pech, wenn uns durch das ewig überholende Schiff der Teller mit Margarine und Butter – im Sommer durch die Wärme flüssig – über Stag ging. Gelegentlich bekamen wir aber eine Flasche Schnaps zum Verscheuern, und sagenhafte Mädchen gab es – beim Kapitän. Und wenn es mit seinem Damenbesuch mal nicht klappte, was selten vorkam, kam er nach vorn ins Mannschaftslogis und lockte die Mädchen in seine Kammer, 'wat wüllt ju bi de Jungs, de hefft doch keen Schnaps und Zigaretten*'!

– if I had, I'd be sailing on a training ship."

He wrote to the Rostock shipowner Fritz Raabe all the same, and asked whether he could sign on as an (unpaid) member of the regular crew. They took him on and he became one of a regular crew of eleven. The owner even employed an engineer to take care of the 125-HP Skandia engine. Wehr was given the post of carpenter and learned how to caulk, operate the anchor capstan and many other things. As ship's lad he had to look after the deck engine in bad weather, which operated the pumps on deck by capillary cable. The wooden ship often leaked 'like a sieve'. The bilge pumps were on deck and most of the time had to be operated manually three times a day, morning, noon and night. Use of the engine was only permitted when the vessel shipped water (which often happened at sea) and manual pumping could no longer cope with the quantities. The food was poor: *"One or two plates of milk soup for breakfast, with or without bread, a bite of lunch and in the evening, sometimes, our luck was out, as the plate with margarine or butter had turned to liquid in the summer heat and would slop over as the ship rolled all the time. Occasionally we'd get a bottle of schnapps to sell and there were fabulous girls – for the old man. When – very occasionally – he failed to get a girl, he'd come into the crew's quarters to entice the girls there into his cabin, with 'What do you want with the boys? They don't have drinks or cigarettes.'*

When he had official visitors the spacious saloon would be cleaned up, we'd be given white jackets to wear and after a quick course of instruction had to serve as waiters. Even our finger nails were clean – as far as that was

Wenn er Gäste hatte, wurde der geräumige Salon herausgeputzt, wir wurden in weiße Jakken gesteckt und mußten uns nach einem Schnellkursus als Servierer betätigen. Sogar unsere Fingernägel waren sauber – soweit wie es möglich war. Nach getaner Arbeit gab er uns großzügig einen Geldschein. Den mußten wir hinterher allerdings wieder abgeben, denn der Alte wollte mit der Großzügigkeit seinen Gästen nur imponieren, aber nicht uns tatsächlich erfreuen. Immerhin blieben uns Reste von der reichhaltigen Tafel. Achtern im Kapitänssalon gab es nämlich Sachen, von denen wir vorn im Logis nur träumen konnten."

Eine durch einen rostigen Nagel verursachte Blutvergiftung führte dann zum Abmustern krankheitshalber. Nicht über die Vergiftung, aber über das Abmustern freute sich Seemann Wehr, das nannte er Glück.

„Ich kam dann auf die SOPHIE aus Barnkrug. Eigner Claus Meyer war 61 Jahre alt, war früher als Matrose auf einem Dampfer gefahren, hatte dann ein kleines Patent gemacht und sich anschließend ein Schiff gekauft. Er war ein sehr erfahrener Seemann, aber die offene See ohne Küstenschutz liebte er nicht, unter Land fühlte er sich sicherer – wohl aufgrund seiner Erfahrungen! Als er anfing, bildete die Fahrt von Unterelbehäfen nach Hamburg die Erwerbsgrundlage. In den Fleeten wurde gestaakt. Nach dem Ersten Weltkrieg hatten die Ewer den Konkurrenzkampf gegen Bahn und Lastkraftwagen verloren. Auch Claus Meyer mußte 'na See hen' fahren, um Geld zu verdienen. Böse Zungen behaupteten, manche Schiffer hätten mit einer Schubkarre gelernt, nach dem Kompaß zu fahren."

Ob das nun so stimmt oder nicht, läßt Oskar Wehr dahingestellt, aber es gab viele von diesem

Ein See-Ewer.
A seagoing ewer.

possible. Once the job was over he would generously slip us a note, which we had to give back to him again, as the old man just wanted to impress his guests, not give us any gratification. All the same there were generous left-overs, as there were things to eat in the saloon which as crew we only dreamt about." When he got blood poisoning from a rusty nail, Oskar Wehr had to sign off sick. Wehr was happy to sign off, not about the blood poisoning. He still considered himself lucky.

"After that I joined the SOPHIE from Barnkrug. Her owner, Claus Meyer, was 61 and had served as an able-bodied seaman on a steamer, had gotten his coastal master's ticket

Schlag Menschen. SOPHIE war als Besanewer getakelt, das laufende Tauwerk oder Gut war geteerter Hanf. Sie war mit einem 25 PS-Glühkopfmotor ausgerüstet und trug 100 Tonnen, wenn die Luke mit einem Herft erhöht wurde, auch 110 Tonnen. Dann glich das Schiff allerdings mehr einem Unterseeboot. Auf diesem Schiff fuhr Oskar Wehr als Leichtmatrose zusammen mit einem Moses. Das Segelsetzen ging so vor sich: Der Schiffsjunge mußte ans Ruder, der Schiffer stopfte sich die Pfeife, stellte sich dann daneben und sagte zu Oskar, 'nun fang an, fang vorne an'.

„Das tat ich, Klüver, Butenklüver, Fock, Großsegel und Besan. Er hat keinen Handschlag mit angelegt, ich mußte alle Segel alleine setzen. Das waren ungefähr 140 Quadratmeter Segel! Sobald wir uns einem Binnengewässer näherten, wie z. B. dem Greifswalder Bodden, wurden auch die Toppsegel gesetzt. Das heißt, ich mußte nochmal alles runterfieren, oben den Takel einscheren, Schot und Hals festsetzen, und wieder alle anderen Segel setzen. Außerdem hatte SOPHIE zwei Schwerter, die auch bedient werden mußten. Aber sonst war es eigentlich ganz gemütlich!"

Die Fahrt war jedenfalls nicht so hart wie auf der DORATHEA. Wie der Schiffer der SOPHIE seinen Leichtmatrosen beurteilte, konnte dieser nicht rausfinden, sein Schiffer grölte immer. Seine 'normale' Anrede war 'Schie Schietkerls', er sprach immer im Plural. Seine Frau kam ab und zu an Bord, sie fuhr nie mit, besuchte ihren Mann aber gelegentlich im Hafen.

„Sie sagte zu uns (dem Schiffsjungen und dem Leichtmatrosen Wehr), laß bloß den Alten schreien und nehmt es nicht so ernst. Wenn ihr mehr Geld braucht, kommt ihr zu mir!"

Der kleine Glühkopfmotor wurde immer benutzt.

and had bought a ship. He was an extremely experienced seaman but disliked the open sea, without the shelter of the shore. He felt safer near the coast, no doubt due to the many bad experiences he had had. Claus Meyer started his career by undergoing basic training between the ports on the lower stretches of the River Elbe and Hamburg. In the city, boats were poled on the canals. After the First World War the traditional wherries lost the race against rail and road transport, so Claus Meyer had to go further afield to make his living. Gossip has it that many skippers had 'used a wheelbarrow' to learn to navigate by compass."

Oskar Wehr never contradicted this statement, but many were in the same situation at the time. The SOPHIE was rigged as a ketch-rigged barge, with rigging of tarred hemp. She had a 25-HP mixed-combustion engine and could carry 100 tonnes – or 110 tonnes with a elevated hatch fitted, whereas she looked like a submarine. Oskar Wehr signed on to the ship as an ordinary seaman along with another deckhand. The procedure for setting sail went as follows: with the deckhand at the wheel and the skipper at his side, filling his pipe, he would tell Oskar to 'Get on with it, start at the fore.'

"So I did: jib, outer jib, foresail, mainsail and jigger. He never gave a hand. I had to set all the sails on my own – about 140 m^2 of canvas! When approaching inland waters like the Greifswalder Bodden the topsails would be set too, which meant I had to lower the whole lot, reeve in the tackle, fasten sheet and tack, then hoist back all the other sails. The SOPHIE had two centreboards which had to be dealt with too. Otherwise things were fairly easy-going."

Der Bug eines Küstenseglers.
The bow of a coastal sailship.

Allerdings hatten die Glühköpfe des Motors es an sich, daß sie häufig kaputt gingen und ersetzt werden mußten.
„Hatten wir nicht genug Reserve-Glühköpfe an Bord, mußten wir segeln, dann blieb uns die Wahl erspart! Vier Meilen, die das Schiff dann in etwa stündlich schaffte. Eines Tages lag das Schiff sommertags auf der Ostsee. Wir beiden Decksgrade nutzten die angenehmen Wassertemperaturen zum Baden. Das merkte der Alte trotz seines Mittagsschlafes, er stürzte schreckensbleich an Deck und tobte: 'Ihr Idioten – ein Windhauch und das Schiff treibt weg, und ich finde euch nicht wieder!"
Das sahen die beiden ein. Das Schiff trieb mit voller Takelage, Wind wehte nicht.

Sailing was not as tough as on the DORATHEA. The seaman had no idea how his skipper could assess his work at all, as he spent his time yelling. He normally addressed the crew as 'You bastards', always using the plural. His wife would come on board occasionally to visit her husband in port, but never sailed with him. *"She told us (the deckhand and Ordinary Seaman Wehr) to 'let the old man yell. Don't take it seriously. If you need more money, come to me.'"*
The mixed-combustion engine was always in use but the ignition bulbs had the habit of breaking down and therefore constantly had to be replaced. *"If we didn't have enough spare bulbs on board we just had to sail – no two ways about it. We did about four knots in roughly an hour. One day the ship was in the Baltic in summer. We deckhands made good use of the warm water and took a swim. The old man saw us, though it was time for his midday snooze. He stormed out on deck shouting 'You idiots – all you need is a breath of wind and the ship'll drift away, then I'll never find you again!"* The young men had to agree. The ship was adrift under full sail with not a breath of wind.
That summer Oskar Wehr told the owner: *"There are bugs on board, Sir."* 'No idea', was the reply, while a fat brown bug crept over the skipper's arm. *"Couldn't you have the ship fumigated, Sir?"* 'Why? They don't bother me,' was the skipper's reply. The SOPHIE was moored alongside a Cords steamer in the port of Rostock. There was a rumour that cockroaches eat bugs. So a bucketful of cockroaches was collected from the steamer's galley and its contents distributed throughout the SOPHIE. First day: no reaction. Sec-

Im Sommer ließ Oskar Wehr gegenüber dem Schiffseigner verlauten:
„Hier sind Wanzen an Bord"
'Weet ick nix vun', sagte er, dabei spazierte eine dicke braune Wanze über seinen Arm.
„Lassen Sie das Schiff doch entgasen", bat Oskar ihn.
'Warum, dat stört mi ni', entgegnete der Schiffer. In Rostock lag SOPHIE dann längsseits von einem Cords-Dampfer. Es ging die Mär um, daß Wanzen von Kakerlaken gefressen werden. Also wurde in der Kombüse des Dampfers eine Pütz Kakerlaken gesammelt und gleichmäßig auf der SOPHIE verteilt. Erster Tag: keine Reaktion. Zweiter Tag: keine Reaktion. Am dritten Tag nicht und am vierten auch nicht. Früher gab es auf der SOPHIE nur Wanzen, jetzt Wanzen <u>und</u> Kakerlaken: das Schiff wurde ausgegast und Wanzen wie Kakerlaken verschwanden.

Ein Jahr war Oskar Wehr an Bord der SOPHIE. Steuern durfte er auch allein, was gelegentlich zu Auseinandersetzungen führte. Wenn das Schiff z. B. vom Nord-Ostsee-Kanal zum Isefjord bestimmt war, fuhr der Schiffer immer durch südlich Langeland und Fünen vorbei zum Kleinen Belt, weil diese Route unter Land führte. Als er auf einer solchen Reise südlich Kjeldsnor das Ruder an den Leichtmatrosen Wehr übergab, um sich unter Deck in die Koje zu begeben, steuerte dieser wie selbstverständlich den Großen Belt an, der Weg war schließlich kürzer. Als der Schiffer den ungewohnten Kurs später bemerkte, reagierte er hysterisch! Auf seinem Schiff bestimme er den Kurs, und der führe immer unter Land! Er fuhr selten durch, d. h. nachts ging er vor Anker, nach dem Motto >Die Nacht ist für die wilden Tiere da<. In der Dunkelheit zu fahren war ihm äußerst unan-

ond day: none at all, nor on the third or fourth. Where the SOPHIE had once been infested by bugs, she now had bugs and cockroaches. The ship was fumigated and an end put to both bugs and roaches.

Oskar Wehr spent a whole year on board the SOPHIE. He was allowed to take the wheel alone, which led to the occasional row. For instance, when his ship was sailing from the Kiel Canal to the Isefjord, the skipper took her south of Langeland, past Fyn and into the Lille Belt, close to shore. On this route Oskar Wehr took over the wheel one day south of Kjeldsnor. The old man went below to get some sleep. Wehr naturally took the shorter route, setting course towards the Store Belt. Later, when the skipper noticed that the ship was on an unfamiliar course his reaction was hysterical. He – the skipper – was the one to set the course on this ship, and always close to shore. The skipper rarely sailed at night, preferring to drop anchor instead, claiming the night was just for wild animals. He intensely disliked sailing in the dark, and only did so if it were unavoidable. If he could, he chose short trips. Part of Wehr's duties included starting the mixed-combustion engine before the anchor was weighed each morning. This often required a great deal of patience. It was one of the most popular jobs in winter, as the bulb had to be heated up first. After a night in a cold bunk one warmed up quickly over the bulb.

Finkenwerder Fischkutter und auf Ladung wartende Küstensegler (im Hintergund) auf der Hamburger Süderelbe.

Finkenwerder trawlers shown with coastal sailships waiting for cargo (far right) on the Süderelbe branch at Hamburg.

genehm. Nur wenn es sich absolut nicht vermeiden ließ, wurde nachts gefahren. Wenn es ging, wählte er Reisen, die 'dicht bei waren'. Zu Wehrs Aufgaben gehörte es, vor dem morgendlichen Ankerlichten den Glühkopfmotor in zu Gang setzen, was oftmals viel Geduld voraussetzte. Im Winter gehörte diese Arbeit zu den beliebtesten, weil man den Glühkopf gut vorwärmen mußte. Nach einer Nacht in der kalten Koje konnte man sich schnell am Glühkopf aufwärmen.

Mitkalkulieren der Frachtergebnisse schon am Anfang

Viel lernen konnte er nicht mehr an Bord der SOPHIE, das meiste kannte und konnte Oskar Wehr schon. Sehr interessant war aber, daß ihm der Schiffer ständig von den Kosten erzählte, die er in den Häfen, für Proviant, die Besatzung und für den Liter Dieselöl (8 Pfennig/Liter) usw. bezahlen mußte. Für diese Zahlen hatte er ein Gedächtnis. Wenn die SOPHIE im Hamburger Ewerhafen lag, dann verwickelte Oskar Wehr die Lehrjungen von Carsten Rehder, bei dem Meyer am Kontor war, in ein Gespräch. So bekam er dann auch mit, welche Frachten sein Schiffer für welche Reisen bekam und kalkulierte. Einzige Unbekannte in dieser Rechnung blieben lange Zeit die Kanalgebühren, deren Höhe er nicht kannte. Die zahlte sein Schiffer im Kanal immer bar, er sprach auch nicht darüber und ausfragen ließ er sich schon gar nicht.

Die Liegezeiten im Ewerhafen mit Warten auf Ladung begrüßten zumindest die Janmaaten. Am Warteplatz befand sich landseitig eine große Schrebergartenkolonie, die ein bevorzugter Aufenthaltsort der Schrebergärtnertöchter zu sein schien. Beide, Töchter und Seeleute, genossen das Leben. *(Außer Schwimmen nichts gewesen).* Die Arbeit war hier am Liegeplatz weniger schwer. Oskar mußte seinen Schiffer morgens mit dem Arbeitsboot quer über die Elbe nach Neumühlen wriggen, von wo der Schiffer zu Fuß ins Kontor von Carsten Rehder stiefelte, um zu hören, ob und welche Ladung es gab. Mittags kam er zum Essen an Bord zurück, um nachmittags wieder ins Kontor zu fahren (das bedeutete dann viermal Wriggen).

Calculations from the start

There was not much more for Oskar Wehr to learn on board the SOPHIE. However he showed a keen interest in what the skipper told him about the expenses which had to be paid in ports – for provisions, crews and diesel oil (8 Pfennig a litre), etc. Whenever the SOPHIE was tied up in the wherry port in Hamburg he talked to the apprentices working at his skipper's shipbrokers, Carsten Rehder. He got to know what freight his owner collected for what voyages and started making his own calculations. Charges for the Kiel Canal remained a mystery to him for a long time, as he never knew their exact amount. The skipper always paid cash; he never talked about the sum and was not disposed to interrogation.

The deckhands at least looked forward to time in the wherry port, waiting for cargo. Ashore there was a group of allotments nearby, where the gardeners' daughters spent their time. Both daughters and sailors enjoyed the life (bathing, no more!). Work at the berth was less strenuous. Every morning Oskar had to scull the skipper across the Elbe to Neumuhlen in the ship's dinghy. From there the master would walk to Carsten Rehder's office to enquire about new cargo. He came back to the ship for lunch, but returned to the office in the afternoon (which meant four sculling trips). This was not because the food on board his own ship was better, but at least it was cheaper and sculling saved money. He could have taken the ferry but that would have cost him 15 Pfennig a trip, even if he could have gotten off right next to the office in Altona.

Zum Mittagessen an Bord kam der Eigner übrigens nicht, weil es hier besser schmeckte, nein, auf dem eigenen Schiff war es auf jeden Fall billiger! Auch das Wriggen sparte Geld. Er hätte auch mit dem Fährdampfer fahren können. Das hätte 15 Pfennige gekostet und er hätte gleich in Altona in unmittelbarer Nähe von Carsten Rehder aussteigen können.

Nächstes Schiff war die KÄTE, eine 1935 von J. J. Sietas gebaute Galeasse mit 147 BRT, 'ein halbmodernes' Schiff, wie sich Wehr erinnert, *„mit dem wir schon etwas mehr machen konnten."* Willy Gerdau aus Neuenfelde war Eigner. Es folgten sechs Monate Fahrzeit als Matrose auf der MARGARETHA NIBBE, einem damals modernen Schiff; die Werft Nobiskrug hatte es erst im Juli 1937 an Heinrich Nibbe aus Cranz geliefert. Das Schiff galt aber als Motorsegler, und das war wichtig. Oskar Wehr fuhr auf diesem mit 194 BRT vermessenen Schiff, um seine Fahrtzeit auf *Segel*schiffen zu komplettieren. Die Matrosenzeit auf Seglern zählte nämlich doppelt in der Berechnung der vor dem Besuch der Steuermannschule notwendigen Fahrenszeit. Richtig gesegelt haben die modernen Schiffe jedoch nicht mehr, sie setzten ihre Plünnen nur, wenn der Wind wirklich genau von achtern blies und ein wenig mitschieben konnte. Die vorhergehenden Schiffe, SOPHIE, BRIGITTE RAABE wie DORATHEA setzten die Segel auch dann, wenn der Wind genau gegenan kam und kreuzten auf 'Teufelkommraus'. KÄTE wie auch MARGARETHA NIBBE fuhren oft auf dem Rhein, bis nach Maxau an der deutsch-französischen Grenze. Dorthin fuhr man Holz, Kohlen oder Getreide, rückkehrend wurden am Rhein Ziegel oder Backsteine für die Ostsee geladen. In die Nordsee steuerten die Schiffe über die Ijssel und die Zuiderzee.

Wehr's next ship was the KÄTE, a galeass of 147 GRT, built in 1935 at the J.J.Sietas shipyard. Wehr remembered it as being 'almost a modern ship, one you could do more with.' It belonged to Willy Gerdau in Neuenfelde. Oskar Wehr then spent six months as an able-bodied seaman on board the MARGARETHA NIBBE. She was modern for her time, and had just been delivered to Heinrich Nibbe in Cranz in July 1937. She was a motor sailer, which was important for Oskar, as he had joined the (194 GRT) ship to complete his obligatory time on sailing ships. Time aboard sailing ships counted double when reckoning the stipulated time at sea before going to nautical college. The newer ships of that type no longer used their sails all the time but only hoisted them when there was an aft wind blowing, which would propel them along. The ships he had been on before, the SOPHIE, the BRIGITTE RAABE and the DORATHEA, had set sail even with a head wind blowing, and therefore had to tack to and fro as best they could. Both the KÄTE and the MARGARETHA NIBBE went on frequent trips on the Rhine – as far as Maxau, on the French border, where the ships would take on timber, coal and grain, loading tiles or bricks at ports on the Rhine for the Baltic. Back in the North Sea the ships would cross the Ijssel and the Zuiderzee.

Küstenmotorschiff MARGARETHA NIBBE (280 tdw/ 1937/oben) und Dampfer AEGIR der Seereederei 'Frigga' AG (6480 tdw/1923/unten) im Nord-Ostsee-Kanal.

Coastal mv MARGARETHE NIBBE (280 tdw/1937/ above) and ss AEGIR of Seereederei 'Frigga' AG (6480 tdw/1923/below) in the Kiel Canal.

Dampfer waren viel größer und komfortabler

Dann kam Oskar Wehr auf einen Dampfer: „Dampfer waren alles, was größer war. Dort gab es geregelte Arbeitszeiten, gute Verpflegung, gute Unterkünfte – auf einem Dampfer war einfach alles besser", schwärmte damals nicht nur der Matrose Wehr. „Nachdem ich bei einer Reederei vorstellig geworden war, gab man mir auf einem Dampfer zwei dicke Drahtenden, die ich spleißen mußte. Ich mühte mich ab, kam aber noch besser voran, als mir der Zimmermann einige gute Tips gab. Als der Spleiß fertig war, wurde ich als Matrose auf dem Dampfer AEGIR der Seereederei 'Frigga' AG angemustert und war einer der Jüngsten an Bord."

Mit diesem Schiff geriet Wehr in den Finnisch-Russischen Krieg. Wenig später strandete der Dampfer vor Eckerö.

„In dieser mißlichen Lage griffen uns russische Flugzeuge an, und die Finnen internierten uns. Mit Gewehrkolben zerstörten sie die Funkbude, da wir trotz Verbots funkten. Wir lagen 18 Kilometer von der Lotsenstation, der nächsten menschlichen Stätte. Draußen waren 40 Grad minus und fünfzig Zentimeter Eisdecke. Das Eis hatte die AEGIR, beladen mit 7500 Tonnen Erz, mittlerweile mit einer dicken Schicht überzogen. Der Kapitän bemühte sich, das Schiff intakt zu halten, aber die Bunkerkohlen wurden immer knapper. Fast alle Leitungen usw. ließen sich entwässern, nur der Kessel selbst nicht. Den beheizten wir mit Holz. Wir bekamen aber nur am Vortage frisch geschnittenes Holz. Der Heizwert war minimal, außerdem mußten die Stämme vom Deckspersonal erst

Steamships – bigger and more comfortable

At last Oskar Wehr joined a steamship: "Steamships meant that everything was bigger and better: regular working hours, good food, and good accommodation." Seaman Wehr was not the only one to be enthusiastic.

"After an interview at a shipping company, they sent me aboard a steamship and handed me two enormous lengths of wire. These I had to splice. It was a hard job but I managed better once the carpenter had given me a few bits of advice. When I'd finished the splicing job I was signed on as an able-bodied seaman aboard the S/S AEGIR, owned by the Frigga AG, an ocean-going shipping line. I was one of the youngest on board."

When on board Wehr became involved in the Russian war against Finland. Shortly thereafter the ship was stranded off Eckerö. "It was an unhappy state of affairs, in which we were attacked by Russian planes and interned by the Finns. They demolished the radio room with their rifle butts because we broke the transmitting prohibition. We were 18 km off the pilot station, the nearest sign of habitation. Outside temperature was around minus 40° C, with ice 50 cm thick. By that time the AEGIR, loaded with 7,500 tonnes of ore, was covered in a thick layer of ice. The master did his best to keep the ship in one piece but we were running out of bunker coal. We managed to drain off all the water pipes except the boiler itself, which we fed with wood. All the wood we got was green, cut fresh the day before. Its heating properties couldn't have been lower. The logs had to be

gesägt, gespalten und über Stellagen an Deck gemannt und vom Maschinenpersonal getrocknet werden. Bei drei Mann Deckspersonal war das Schwerstarbeit, aber die Offiziere halfen uns. Zur Sicherung des Schiffes wurden von der gesamten Besatzung die beiden Buganker nach Steuerbordseite ausgefahren (etwa 200 m). Mittels selbstgebauter Schlitten gelang diese Arbeit nach großer Mühe. Nach dem Friedensschluß riß uns der Eisbrecher SAMPO los. nachdem wir inzwischen 2500 Tonnen Erz aus dem Laderaum geschaufelt hatten. 'Wir' bedeutete jedoch nur noch die halbe Besatzung von 17 Mann, die andere Hälfte hatte gemeutert. Sie wurden abgesondert und, nachdem wir wieder flott waren, über Schweden nach Deutschland gebracht und bestraft."

Inzwischen befand sich das Deutsche Reich im Krieg und Wehr wurde, wie unzählige andere auch, dienstverpflichtet. Er kam auf den französischen Frachter CAPITAINE LE BASTARD, ein Schiff, um das sich dessen privater Eigner sehr sorgte. Mit diesem Schiff ging es eines Tages von Nantes nach Le Havre, aber vor dem Einlaufen in den Englischen Kanal blieb das Schiff liegen: der Generatormotor des Mineneigenschutzes (MES) hatte seinen Geist aufgegeben, die Folge eines Sabotage-Aktes. Der Kapitän wartete auf Anweisungen (ohne MES durfte der minenverseuchte Kanal nicht befahren werden), Oskar Wehr stand am Ruder, gebannt suchte man die Wasseroberfläche nach der drohenden U-Boot-Gefahr ab. Rudergänger Wehr lästerte über den Motor – um dessen Wiederbelebung sich der ebenfalls dienstverpflichtete Chief vergeblich bemüht hatte, solange, bis der Kapitän nachgab: 'Dann wollen mir mal sehen, ob Du den Motor wie-

sawn, chopped and carried across duckboards set up on deck. Then they were dried by the engine crew. With only three deck's crew, this was hard work, but we were helped by the officers. The whole crew helped drop both the bow anchors to starboard (about 200 metres) in an effort to secure the ship. With great effort we managed, using homemade sledges. Following the Peace Treaty we were freed by the icebreaker SAMPO, after we had shovelled some 2,500 tonnes of ore from the hold. 'We' in this case meant half of the crew of 17. The other half had mutinied. They were put into detention and once we were afloat again, sent back to Germany, via Sweden, where they were disciplined."

By that time Germany was at war and, like countless others, Wehr was called up. He joined the French freighter CAPITAINE LE BASTARD, which was owned by a Frenchman who looked after her meticulously. On one trip the ship was sailing from Nantes to Le Havre but had to stop before reaching the English Channel because the generator motor on the demagnetisation unit was defunct, having been sabotaged. The Captain awaited instructions, as the mine-riddled Channel was not navigable without demagnetisation equipment. Oskar Wehr was at the wheel, while everyone concentrated on scanning the surface of the water for submarines. Wehr kept complaining about the motor, which the chief engineer - a conscript like Wehr – had tried to resuscitate in vain, until the master cut in: 'Well, let's see if you can get her going again.' It was definitely worth a try in such an uncomfortable situation and, having served on a coaster, constant trouble with ignition bulbs was nothing new to Wehr. So Wehr requested

Zwei Kriegstransporter begegnen sich im Mittelmeer *Two military transports passing in the Mediterranean.*

der in Schwung bekommst'. Einen Versuch in der mißlichen Lage war es allemal wert, denn den Leuten von Klütenewern der Küstenschiffahrt war der laufende Ärger mit den Lagern der Glühköpfe nichts Neues. Wehr forderte Männer und Material an: eine Mettwurst, zwei dicke Seiten Speck, eine Flasche Schnaps, den Storekeeper als üblicherweise bestausgebildeten Mann an Bord und einen Hilfsmann. Das kaputte Lager wurde ausgebaut, die Speckscheiben eingepaßt, und so kam der Frachter mit funktionierendem Mineneigenschutz bis zum nächsten Hafen.

Für den Besuch der Steuermannsschule fehlte Oskar Wehr noch ein Teil des nötigen Geldes. Das verdiente er sich im Hamburger Hafen, vor allem in der Nachtschicht, die mit 16 Mark

men and material: a sausage, two large sides of bacon, a bottle of schnapps, the storekeeper (as the best trained member of the crew), and another hand to help. The broken bearing was removed and replaced with the bacon. The freighter made it to the next port with her demagnetisation equipment in working order.

As Oskar Wehr still did not have enough money to attend nautical college, he worked in the Port of Hamburg, mainly at nights, where he earned 16 Marks per night. He had done this before, while waiting for orders on board small ships, improving his wages with the proceeds of a night's shift. As many of his colleagues stayed up on the spree all night, come the morning everyone was tired, if for different reasons.

bezahlt wurde. Schon früher, wenn er mit einem der Klütenewer im Hamburger Hafen lag und auf irgendwelche Order wartete, hatte er seinen Lohn mit der Früchten einer Nachtschicht verbessert. Viele Kameraden feierten die Nacht durch, müde waren alle – aus unterschiedlichen Gründen.

Während des Krieges verlor Oskar Wehr sechs Schiffe, drei auf See und drei im Hafen, durch U-Boote, Fliegerbomben, Minen und Artillerie. „Auch bei den Italienern machte ich mich beliebt", erzählt Wehr,
„und sollte die Medaille 'Dascento' erhalten, die mit dem Deutschen Kreuz in Gold zu vergleichen war. Auf die Frage, was ich von Beruf sei, antwortete ich mit 'Aspirante delle Offiziale de Peroskafe!', einer Position (dem Offiziersaspiranten), die in Italien ungleich höher angesiedelt war, als bei uns, weil er schon ein studierter Mann war. Ich war kein Offizier, und mein Kapitän Bründel sollte den Orden statt meiner bekommen, was dieser ablehnte. Der eingeschaltete deutsche Admiral suchte händeringend nach einer Lösung, denn brüskieren wollte man die verbündeten Italiener nicht."

Alle waren zur Ordensverleihung angetreten, aber Kapitän Bründel wollte und wollte nicht. Er war einer der bekanntesten Kapitäne des Zweiten Weltkrieges, er hatte die ANKARA mit von Generalfeldmarschall Rommel dringend benötigem Nachschub dreizehn mal nach Afrika gebracht und wieder zurück, das war Rekord. Er war Träger des Eisernen Kreuzes I und II sowie des Deutschen Kreuzes in Gold. Er war ein honoriger Mann mit viel Mut. Wenn er in eine Kneipe kam, grüßten ihn – den Zivilisten – Marineangehörige unabhängig von ihrem Rang. Der Admiral fragte den Matrosen Wehr,

During the War six of the ships on which Oskar Wehr served were lost due to attacks by submarines, air raids, mines and shelling. Three were lost at sea, three in port. *"I got popular with the Italians,"* Oskar Wehr remembers, *"and I was to get the 'Dascento' medal, the same as the Deutsches Kreuz in Gold (the highest medal awarded to civilians). When asked my profession, I said 'Aspirante delle Offiziale de Peroskafe!', which was a much higher status in Italy than in Germany, as one had to be a graduate first. I was a rating, so the Captain was to receive the decoration in my stead. But he declined. The German admiral involved racked his brains to find a solution to the problem without snubbing the Italians."*
Everyone attended for the decoration ceremony, but Captain Bründel still refused. As master he had one of the best reputations in the Second World War, as he had brought Field Marshall Rommel reinforcements to North Africa and back in the ANKARA thirteen times - a record. He had been awarded both classes of the Iron Cross and the Deutsches Kreuz in Gold. He was a man of honour and courage (when he went into a pub all the naval men would salute him – as a civilian – irrespective of rank). The admiral asked Seaman Wehr what his real objective was. 'Study leave, Sir'. That solved the problem. Captain Bründel accepted the medal and Wehr was given study leave - in writing. On his trip from Naples to Hamburg men in uniform constantly tried to get him sent back to the front. He eventually got to Hamburg and nautical college, if a day later than planned. He had to spend a night in prison in Würzburg, because his orders were issued for Hamburg but he

was er denn wolle, worauf ein zackiges 'Studienurlaub, Herr Admiral' kam. Das war die Lösung, Kapitän Bründel nahm den Orden an, Wehr bekam Studienurlaub, und den sogar schriftlich. Uniformierte Menschen versuchten zwar auf seiner Reise von Neapel nach Hamburg mehrfach, ihn wieder an die Front zu schicken, aber er kam schließlich in Hamburg in der Seefahrtsschule an, wenn auch nach eintägiger Unterbrechung. In Würzburg hatte er eine Nacht eingesessen, sein Marschbefehl lautete nämlich auf Hamburg, er saß aber im Zug nach Koblenz.

„Ich wollte meine Sachen holen, schließlich hatte ich keine Lust, im Segelpäckchen in der Schule anzutreten!"

was found on train for Koblenz. "I was only getting my things. I didn't want to start school in sailing gear."

Die Schiffsführung des Dampfers MAR DEL PLATA (vrnl): Funkinspektor Blasse, Ltd. Ingenieur Steffens, Kapitän Freudenberg und der III. Offizier Oskar Wehr in Zivil.

Ship's command of ss MAR DEL PLATA (from right): Radio Superintendent Blasse, Chief Engineer Steffens, Captain Freudenberg, and Third Mate Oskar Wehr in civvies.

Anstellung als Offizier und ein Entschluß

Oskar Wehr brauchte keine vier Semester für sein Patent A 5, nach 13 Monaten Schule hatte er es, exakt am 12. Juni 1943. Sein erstes Schiff als junger Offizier war die MAR DEL PLATA, ein ehemals belgisches Fracht- und Passagierschiff der Cie. Maritime Belge SA in Antwerpen. Das 7340 BRT große und 132,85 m lange Schiff war erst am 17. September 1938 von John Cockerill in Hoboken abgeliefert worden. Das schnelle Schiff verfügte über umfangreiche Kühlräume, fuhr unter der Reichsdienstflagge und wurde personell von der Hamburg-Süd betreut.

„Das erste Gespräch an Bord in der Messe hat mich derart erschüttert, daß alle meine Illusionen verflogen. Schöne Uniform, tolle Kammern- der Traum dahin. Der eine Offizier erzählte, daß er sechs Jahre fahren mußte, bis er seinen Hausstand zusammen hatte, der nächste brauchte noch länger für sein Ziel, und alle sprachen von langen Fahrtzeiten, bis die nächste Beförderungsstufe erreicht war. Um die 125 Mark verdiente der Dritte Offizier plus einige Zulagen. Das fand ich gar nicht so erstrebenswert. Ich dachte zurück an meine Küstenschiffskapitäne. Sie mußten zwar mehr arbeiten, verdienten aber viel mehr, das wußte ich ja noch von meinen Nachkalkulationen. Ich faßte den Entschluß, Küstenschiffer zu werden!"

Zugute kam ihm die umfassende Ausbildung aus der Küstenschifferzeit. Die Bestätigung dafür erhielt er als Matrose in der Dampferzeit. Wenn ein Heizer ausfiel, schaute die Schiffsführung die Seefahrtsbücher durch und dann hieß es >Wehr, du hest op'n Klütenewer fohrt, du kennst

Officer and Shipowner

Oskar Wehr took less than two years to get his coastal shipping Captain's license – in fact it took him exactly thirteen months of studies, as he received it on 12th June 1943. His first ship as a junior officer was the MAR DEL PLATA, formerly a combination freighter and passenger ship belonging to the Compagnie Maritime Belge S.A. of Antwerp. The ship had 7,340 GRT, was 132.85m long and had just been built by the John Cockerill yard in Hoboken on 17th September 1938. She was a fast ship, with a large capacity for refrigerated cargo and sailed under the official German ensign. She was managed by the Hamburg-Süd shipping company.

"My first conversation in the mess room shattered any illusions I'd had. In spite of grand uniforms and luxurious cabins, the dream was over. One officer recounted how he'd had to go to sea for six years before he'd saved up enough to set up house. Another had taken even longer. All of them, however, knew that they had to go to sea for extremely long periods before being promoted. A third officer earned 125 Marks plus a few extras. This was not what I had been aiming for. I remembered the skippers I'd had on the coastal ships. They'd had to work harder but they earned a lot more. I knew this from all the calculations I'd made. That was when I decided to become a short sea skipper."

All the training he had had on coastal vessels now paid dividends. This had become evident when he worked on steamships as an ordinary seaman. If a stoker had to be replaced, the master would look through the seaman's books before saying:"Wehr, you served on a coaster,

Helga und Oskar Wehr 1943 (links oben). Oskar Wehr (rechts) und Offiziersanwärter Gärtner auf einem Mittelmeerdampfer (darunter). Deutsche und italienische Kriegskameraden auf MAR DEL PLATA (rechts oben) und Angriff auf einen Mitelmeertransport (darunter).

Helga und Oskar Wehr in 1943 (above left). (Below:) Oskar Wehr (right) on a Mediterranean steamer with petty officer Gärtner. German and Italian comrades aboard ss MAR DEL PLATA (above right). A Mediterranean transport under attack (below).

wat vun de Maschin, du gost nu rünner in unse Maschin.< Ähnlich war es, wenn der Koch nicht da war, auch Kochen lernte man sehr schnell auf einem Klütenewer. Die Überführung einer sogenannten Siebelfähre nach Derna hatte man ihm während des Krieges anvertraut. Alle angesprochenen Offiziere waren unabkömmlich und Derna lag mitten im Kriegsgebiet. Auch Frau Helga Wehr befand den Entschluß, Küstenschiffer zu werden, für gut, obwohl sie – aus einer alten Küstenschifferfamilie stammend – eigentlich keinen Seemann heiraten wollte. Kennengelernt hatten sich die beiden am 8. Mai 1942, dem Tag, an dem Oskar Wehr seinen A 5-Lehrgang antrat.

you know about engines. Down into the engine room with you." The same thing happened when there was no cook, because cooking was one of the things one had to learn on a small ship. During the War Wehr was instructed to take the 'Siebel ferry' (as it was called) to Derna. All other officers were indisposed and Derna was in a fighting area.

Helga Wehr also concurred with his decision to become a coastal skipper, in spite of the fact that she came from a family of coastal shippers and had never wanted to marry a seaman. They had met on 8th May 1942, the day Oskar Wehr had sat the examination for his coastal Captain's license.

Die Familie Selmer von der Insel Sylt

Helga Wehr geborene Selmer stammt aus der alten Seefahrerfamilie Selmer. Thomas Selmer erhielt 1866 die Konzession, Post und Passagiere nach Sylt zu befördern, nachdem die 1859 gegründete Sylter Dampfschiffs-Gesellschaft mit ihrem Dampfer IDA gescheitert war. Selmer erwarb den Dampfer WILHELM, der sich jedoch bald als zu klein erwies. Als Ersatz kam der extrem flachgehende Heckraddampfer BISMARCK, der jedoch – vor allem bei Sturm – nicht besonders seetüchtig war. 1873 fuhr die BISMARCK aufgrund einer Wette nach Tondern, konnte im engen Tonderaner Hafen auf der Wiedau nicht drehen und mußte bis Hoyer, dem eigentlichen Festlandshafen, rückwärts fahren, was Tonderaner Seminaristen zum Verfassen eines Spottliedes bewog:

In der großen Seestadt Tondern
kam jüngst mal ein Dampfschiff an;
alle Leute tun sich wundern,
daß man hier auch schiffen kann.
Mann und Weib und Kind und Wesen
eilen nach der Schiffbrück hin,
um zu sehn, was nie gewesen,
wie das Dampfschiff kommt dahin.
Voll Verwunderung steht die Menge
gafft die schmutz'ge Bismarck an.
Ach! Fest sitzt sie in der Enge,
daß man sie nicht retten kann.
Seht auf Tonderns weise Väter
wie sie sich beraten drum,
daß sie diesen Schwerenöter
kriegen in dem Hafen rum.
'Hängt ihn' sprach der eine weise,
'hängt ihn in den Kran hinein!'

The Selmer Family from Sylt

Helga Wehr's maiden name was Selmer, a seafaring family of long standing. In 1866 Thomas Selmer was granted a licence to carry mail and passengers to the island of Sylt because the Sylter Dampfschiffs-Gesellschaft, founded in 1859, had failed to provide successful services with the IDA. Selmer began by buying the WILHELM, but it soon proved too small. It was replaced by the shallow-draft sternwheeler BISMARCK, but she proved unseaworthy, particularly in stormy weather. In 1873 the BISMARCK sailed to Tondern, on the River Wiedau, as part of a bet. However the port basin in Tondern was so narrow, she had to sail all the way to Hoyer in reverse, the main port on the mainland. Even students in Tondern wrote a satirical poem about the incident.

Thomas Selmer

Und ein andrer sagte leise:
'Grabt ein Loch ins Ufer rein!'
Seht sie drängen, seht sie schieben,
doch die lange BISMARCK spricht:
'Leut, es tut mir nicht belieben,
rum zu kriegen bin ich nicht!'
Da ruft einer aus im Zorne:
'Rückwärts laßt ihn Tondern fliehen,
kam er auch herein von vorne,
rückwärts laßt ihn wieder ziehen'.
Die Moral von der Geschicht,
höret wie ein Weiser spricht:
'Wo du nicht heraus kannst kommen,
da hinein begib dich nicht!'

Thomas Selmer hatte jedoch bald keine Lust mehr, für die 'hochwohlgeborenen Kurgäste' und die Sylter bei jedem Wetter, aber kargem Lohn, die Fährverbindung zu verrichten. Er verkaufte seine Konzession und sein Schiff an den Ziegeleibesitzer Clausen. Immerhin hatten alle aus BISMARCKS Fahrt nach Tondern gelernt. Der 1882 von Howaldt in Kiel gebaute Seitenraddampfer NORDSEE (129 BRT), der auch

Thomas Selmer soon tired of ferrying 'high-class' passengers and the inhabitants of Sylt back and forth to the island in all weathers, at low prices. So he sold both licence and ship to Mr Clausen, a brickworks owner. By that time the BISMARCK's trip to Tondern had taught everyone a lesson. The side-paddle-steamer NORDSEE (129 GRT) had been built at the Howaldt dockyard in Kiel in 1882, to run services to Tondern. She was the only North Sea steamer which looked the same from both ends and had two steering columns. She was able to negotiate the Wiedau forwards or backwards without any trouble. Mementos of Thomas Selmer, the post ship captain, can still be seen at the museum in Keitum.

Hugo Ingwer Selmer was one of Selmer's three sons – the others being Bertram and Wilhelm – but the only one to go to sea. He borrowed 10,000 gold Marks from his father in 1905 and bought a yacht with a 100- tonne capacity. With it he carried coal from the Firth

Hoyerschleuse: Zur Abfahrt nach Sylt/Westerland bereit.   *Hoyerschleuse: Ready for depature to Sylt/Westerland.*

Tondern bedienen sollte, sah als einziges Seedampfschiff an der Nordsee vorn und hinten gleich aus, und hatte außerdem zwei Ruderstände. Er konnte die Wiedau gleichermaßen vor- und rückwärts befahren. Im Museum von Keitum hängen heute noch Erinnerungsstücke an den Postdampferkapitän Selmer. Hugo Ingwer Selmer war einer der drei Söhne Selmers und der einzige, der zur See fuhr. Die beiden anderen hießen Bertram und Wilhelm. Mit vom Vater 1905 geliehenen 10.000 Goldmark kaufte er sich eine rund 100 Tonnen tragende Yacht, mit der er Kohle vom schottischen Firth of Forth nach Munkmarsch brachte. Da er diesen kleinen am nördlichen Ostufer Sylts gelegenen Hafen nur bei Springflut anlaufen konnte, mußte er in List löschen und die Kohle per Pferdefuhrwerk auf der Insel verteilen, was den Erlös der für eigene Rechnung verkauften Kohle schmälerte. Kurz vor dem ersten Weltkrieg ließ er sich von Bodewes in Martenshoek für 15.000 Goldmark den Plattbodenschoner MIMI bauen, der mit Seitenschwertern speziell für seine Erfordernisse konstruiert war. In den zwanziger Jahren verdiente er so gut, daß er sich mehrere Häuser bauen konnte. Als er bei Peters in Wewelsfleth einen Callesen-Motor einbauen lassen wollte, fiel dieser in den Raum. Hugo Selmer war so verärgert, daß er vom Vorhaben der Motorisierung absah und sein Schiff gegen ein anderes, größeres mit einem anderen Eigner 'schlicht um schlicht' tauschte. Es handelte sich um die 1912 in Stadskanaal gebaute Kufftjalk MIMI SELMER ex GLÜCKAUF von 101 BRT, die er am 8.2.1924 in das Schiffsregister von Hamburg eintragen ließ. Im Oktober 1926 ließ er in Glückstadt dann doch einen Callesen-Motor einbauen, der aber nur so lange störungsfrei lief, wie ein Werksmonteur aus Aabenraa

of Forth in Scotland to Munkmarsch. As this small port, on the north-east coast of Sylt, could only be reached on a spring tide, the vessel had to be discharged in List and the coal taken round the island by horse-drawn cart at his own expense. This, of course, reduced the profit margin.

Shortly before the First World War he had a flat-bottomed schooner built for 15,000 gold Marks at the Bodewes yard in Martenshoek - the MIMI. She was specially equipped with leeboards to suit his requirements. By the 1920s he had earned enough to build a number of houses. However, an order with the Peters yard in Wewelsfleth to fit a Callesen engine into the ship ended with the engine dropping down into the hold. Hugo Selmer was so annoyed that it put him off plans for motorisation altogether and, in a straight swap with another owner, he exchanged the ship for a slightly larger one, the tjalk MIMI SELMER (formerly the 101 GRT GLÜCKAUF), which had been built in Stadskanaal in 1912. She was registered in Hamburg on 8th February 1924. In spite of his experience, in 1926 Selmer had the ship fitted with a Callesen engine in Glückstadt, which only operated satisfactorily as long as a fitting engineer from Aabenraa was on board. On 5th/6th December the same year Selmer lost the MIMI SELMER. During a storm she sprang a leak on a trip from Copenhagen to Aalborg with a cargo of maize. The skipper went down with her.

The occurrence caused Mimi Selmer, Hugo's wife, to demand he give up shipping. Instead they bought a tavern for seamen in Hamburg. To this day 'Ida and Hugo's' reputation is legendary in the seafaring and student community. The pub closed in the 1970s. How-

Um 1904 erwarb Hugo Selmer die Yacht ANNE, die er 1914 für die MIMI SELMER (unten) in Zahlung gab. Das Bild zeigt sie unmittelbar nach Ablieferung in Delfzijl.

Hugo Selmer bought the yacht ANNE around 1904 and traded her in for the MIMI SELMER (below) in 1914, shown here immediately after delivery at Delfzijl.

an Bord war. Am 5./6. Dezember 1926 verlor er sein Schiff. Auf einer Reise mit Mais von Kopenhagen nach Aalborg sprang MIMI SELMER im Sturm leck, Hugo Selmer verlor Schiff und Steuermann.

Ehefrau Mimi verlangte von Ehemann Hugo die Aufgabe der Seefahrt, im Hamburg wurde eine 'Wirtschaft für Schiffer' gekauft. Diese Kneipe ist heute noch unter Seeleuten und Seefahrtsschülern unter dem Begriff 'bei Ida und Hugo' eine Legende. Leider exisitiert sie seit den siebziger Jahren nicht mehr. In dieser Schifferkneipe hatte Hugo natürlich dauernden Kontakt mit anderen Schiffern, vor allem mit solchen aus Haren an der Ems. Das waren tüchtige Schiffer, sie liebten aber mehr die Kanäle und Flüsse. Wenn sie bei entsprechendem Wasserstand mit Stückgut vom Rhein nach Berlin fuhren, überließen sie ihr Schiff gegen gutes Salär Hugo Selmer, der es von der Ems bis zu den Hamburger Oberelbebrücken brachte. Kapitän Hugo Selmer hielt es an Land nicht aus, er nahm jede Kapitänsvertretung an, bei Frieseckes, die aus der Binnenschiffahrt stammten, war er zwei Jahre. 1956 fuhr er dann noch als Kapitän auf dem 282 BRT-Betonschiff MODAG, dessen Eigner sein Patent verloren hatte. Wohl fühlt er sich auf dem 'Zementkasten' allerdings nicht, er starb im Alter von 80 Jahren vor Erreichen von Malmö an Bord. In einem in die deutsche Flagge gehüllten Zinksarg wurde er auf dem Achterdeck der MODAG nach Travemünde überführt. Hunderte von Menschen waren Zeugen der Ausschiffung des Sarges. Es war im Sinne des Kapitäns, denn wenn er heimwärts das Lister Tief passiert hatte, setzte er immer die Sylter Flagge zum Zeichen, daß er froh war, es wieder einmal geschafft zu haben. Die Beerdigung fand in Hamburg statt,

ever, it kept Hugo in touch with other skippers, particularly those from Haren on the Ems. They were all experienced skippers, but with a preference for canals and rivers. If water-levels were right, they would take general cargo from the Rhine to Berlin, handing over their ships to Hugo (for good remuneration) for the stretch from the Ems to the bridges of the upper Elbe in Hamburg. Hugo Selmer was unable to stay ashore. He took on any relief job as skipper and was with the Frieseckes, originally an inland waterway company, for two years. In 1956 he captained the 282 GRT concrete-carrier MODAG, whose owner had lost his licence. Hugo did not feel at ease on the 'concrete box' and he died aboard her at the age of 80, before they could reach Malmö. In a zinc coffin covered in a German flag, his body was taken to Travemünde on the deck of the MODAG. Hundreds of people witnessed the coffin being taken ashore.

Hugo und Mimi Selmer, Tochter Ida und ihr Sohn Claus, links eine Besucherin.

Hugo and Mimi Selmer, daughter Ida and her son Claus, and a visitor (from right).

die ganze Familie war vertreten. Unzählige alte und junge Kapitäne, Makler, Verbandsvertreter und Ausrüster gaben ihm die letzte Ehre auf seiner letzten Fahrt. Er war überall beliebt und galt als besonders tüchtiger Segelküstenschiffskapitän.

The ceremony would have pleased Selmer. Every time he passed the Lister Tief on a journey home he would hoist the Sylt flag as a token of thanks for his safe return. The funeral was in Hamburg. It was attended by the whole family. Countless captains, young and old, shipbrokers, members of various associations and ship chandlers all paid him their last respects. He had been a popular, experienced master on coastal sailing ships.

Kapitän Hugo Selmer mit seiner Frau Mimi und Tochter Helga auf der MIMI SELMER.

Captain Hugo Selmer with his wife, Mimi and their daughter, Helga, on the MIMI SELMER.

Vor Selmers Gastwirtschaft: vlnr, hintere Reihe: Ilse Länger, Mimi Selmer, Hugo Selmer, Annegret Schümann, Oskar Wehr, Tante Bertha, Helga Wehr, eine Besucherin (halb verdeckt), Frieda Boll (Helga Wehrs Schwester). Vorne: Inge Boll, Peter Nagel, Elke Boll und Lene Nagel.

A family gathering outside Hugo Selmer's pub, (left to right, back row) Ilse Länger, Mimi Selmer, Hugo Selmer, Annegret Schümann, Oskar Wehr, Aunt Bertha, Helga Wehr, a visitor (partly concealed), Frieda Boll (sister of Helga Wehr). Front row: Inge Boll, Peter Nagel, Elke Boll, Lene Nagel.

Junge Ehe in schwierigen Zeiten

Am 9. September 1944 hatte das Ehepaar Wehr geheiratet. Die Wohnung in einer Parallelstraße der Palmaille war das Opfer eines Bombentreffers geworden. Oskar Wehr war 1942 see- und kriegsuntauglich geschrieben worden. Er litt unter Malaria, fuhr nach Erlangung seines Patentes dennoch wieder zur See – die Personalknappheit war damals sehr groß. Das lange Schwimmen im Wasser (nach den Untergängen) hatte tiefe Spuren hinterlassen. Un-

Young marriage – hard times

The Wehrs were married on 9th September 1944. Their flat in a street parallel to Palmaille had been destroyed by bombs during the war. In 1942 Oskar Wehr was declared unfit for war service at sea as he suffered from malaria. In spite of this he returned to sea once he had obtained his licence, due to the scarcity of seamen at the time. Having to swim for his life – often for long periods – when the ships he was on sank, had left its mark. He

So wie hier an den Vorsetzen sah es auch wenige hundert Meter weiter am Meßberg aus, Wracks und Ruinen überall im Hamburger Hafen.

The postwar Hamburg portscape, seen here at Vorsetzen and identical a few hundred metres upriver at Messberg: wrecks, ruins, debris.

mittelbar nach der Kapitulation am 8. Mai 1945 begann die Suche nach dem eigenen Küstenschiff. Das war angesichts der damaligen unsicheren Verhältnisse sehr schwierig. Oskar Wehr erfuhr, daß unten im Hamburger Hafen am Meßberg ein Schiff läge – allerdings vier Meter unter Wasser. Über einen freundlichen Makler kam man an den Eigner. Carsten Raap hatte die ANNE – so hieß das Wrack – 1906 von J. Sietas in Cranz bauen lassen, er selbst war 68 Jahre alt und wollte sich zur Ruhe setzen. Die Ausbildung zum Rettungsschwimmer und die Zeit als Bademeister in der Seefahrtschule zahlte sich für Oskar Wehr nun aus. Er konnte tauchen und sich sein künftiges Schiff selbst ansehen. Das durch einen Bombentreffer in den

started looking out for a coaster as soon as the War ended on 8th May 1945.
It was not an easy task in such unsettled times. Oskar Wehr got word of a ship which was lying in the port of Hamburg, near Messberg – four metres below the water. Through a helpful shipbroker he traced down its owner as being Carsten Raap. He had had the ANNE (as the wreck was named) built for him in 1906 by J.J.Sietas in Cranz. At the age of 68 Raap had decided to retire. Oskar Wehr's training as a lifesaver and pool attendant at the nautical college now paid off. He knew how to dive, so was able to inspect his prospective ship himself. A horse and cart could have gone through the shelled hole in

Rumpf gerissene Loch war allerdings so groß, daß Pferd und Wagen hätten hindurchfahren können. Ein großer Teil der Ladung Kohl befand sich noch im Raum, einige Köpfe davon lagen um das Schiff herum. Nun fing die Handelei an, 10.000 Mark, bankmäßig nachzuweisendes Geld, hatte Wehr angespart, aber 15.000 Mark wollte Raap auf Basis 'as she is, where is' haben. Und zwar 5000 Reichsmark sofort, und 10.000 Mark in der neuen Währung. Diese Verhandlungen begannen im August 1945 (!), aber daß eine neue Währung kommen mußte, war allen Beteiligten klar. Runterhandeln ließ Carsten Raap sich nicht, und andere Tonnage, die man kaufen konnte, war auch nicht in Sicht. Man griff zu. Dr. Dabelstein setzte einen Vertrag auf, die Umschreibungsformalitäten im Schiffsregister Stade wurden erledigt und im Herbst 1945 war Oskar Wehr sowohl Schiffseigner wie auch noch angestellter Zweiter Offizier der ehemaligen deutschen Kriegsmarine. Für 2500 Mark hob Taucher Flint das Wrack und brachte es zur Schiffswerft Grube in Warwisch. Der junge Schiffseigner hatte es zu dieser Werft schaffen lassen, weil er annahm, Oberelbewerften seien billiger als Hamburger Werften. Aber die Werft war garnicht an der Reparatur interessiert, sondern hatte das Schiff nur ausschlachten wollen. Wehr wiederum hatte nur einen Gedanken, nämlich den, so schnell wie möglich Geld mit dem Schiff zu verdienen. Dazu aber mußten die Schäden erst repariert sein. Zusammen mit dem von Föhr stammenden Andreas Petersen hat Oskar Wehr dann im Schlamm den Motor auseinandergebaut und zum Hersteller der Jastram-Motorenfabrik in Bergedorf gebracht.

„Dann habe ich Herbert Wolkau kennen- und liebengelernt".

the hull. A fair amount of cargo (cabbage) was still in the hold and some strewn round the vessel. The bargaining began. Wehr had banked savings of 10,000 Marks but Raap asked for 15,000 Marks on an 'as is – where is', basis. This meant a down-payment of 5,000 Reichsmark, the balance of 10,000 to be paid in the new currency. Negotiations commenced in August of 1945. Both parties knew the currency reform was coming but not when. In spite of many attempts, Wehr was unable to beat the price down. No other vessel was in the offing. So the deal was closed. The lawyer Dr. Dabelstein drew up a contract for the sale and the ship was transferred to Oskar Wehr in the Stade registry. By the autumn of 1945 Wehr became a shipowner, and was still second mate of the former German navy. Flint, a diver, raised the wreck and took it to the Grube shipyard at Warwisch, charging 2,500 Marks. The young shipowner had chosen the shipyard as he assumed it would cost less to have his ship repaired on the upper Elbe than in Hamburg. The yard was only interested in cannibalising the wreck. Wehr's interest, on the other hand, was only to start earning money as soon as possible. That meant having the ship repaired first. With his friend Andreas Petersen from Föhr, Oskar Wehr dismantled the engine while it was still in the mud and took it to the Jastram engine factory in Bergedorf.

"That was where I met – and learned to respect - Herbert Wolkau." In 1942 Wolkau had taken over the small shipyard on the Reiherstieg founded by his grandfather in 1860. He was prepared to carry out good repairs for the young shipowner and was angry when he discovered that vital parts

ANNE vor der Verlängerung im Hamburger Hafen. *The ANNE prior to lengthening, in the port of Hamburg.*

Er hatte 1942 die kleine, 1860 von seinem Großvater gegründete Werft am Reiherstieg übernommen und war bereit, dem jungen Reeder eine ordentliche Reparatur zu liefern. Zornig wurde Wolkau, als er sah, welche Bauteile der ANNE sich auf der Warwischer Werft schon verflüchtigt hatten. „Du baust jetzt zwei Schotten ein (damit das Schiff Festigkeit bekam) und dann bringen wir es zu mir", befand Wolkau. Gesagt, getan, Herbert Wolkau schleppte, Oskar Wehr fuhr zum ersten Mal auf seinem eigenen Schiff (allerdings im Schlepp), hatte aber große Bedenken, ob es den Reiherstieg heil erreichen würde.

„Wolkau war ein netter Kerl, er half gern jun-

from the ANNE had vanished at the Warwisch yard. *"Have two bulkheads fitted to give her stability, then bring her round to me."* No sooner said than done. Herbert Wolkau towed the ANNE with Oskar Wehr on board his first own ship, in spite of qualms as to whether they would reach Reiherstieg safely. *"Wolkau was a nice chap. He used to help young people and say 'God help the seaman in distress, but steering's your own responsibility. I'll help you where I can.'"*

Repairing the ship was not the only problem, guarding it also took up time. People could use anything and everything in 1946. The shipyard workers helped themselves to pieces

gen Leuten. Er sagte Gott hilft dem Seemann in der Not, steuern mußt Du selbst. Ick schoster di to, wat ick kreegn kann!"

Es mußte jedoch nicht nur am Schiff gearbeitet werden, auch die Bewachung nahm viel Zeit in Anspruch. Gebrauchen konnte man damals – 1946 – alles. Die Werftarbeiter fingen an, und machten u.a. aus kleinen Eisenplatten der ANNE Hexen, das waren kleine Öfen, auf denen man auch kochen konnte. Wehr sann auf Abhilfe und fand sie. Ehemalige Schulkollegen und ehemalige Offiziere sprachen den Jungreeder an. Sie machten zwar gute Schwarzmarktgeschäfte, brauchten aber einen Arbeitsnachweis, den sie normalerweise nur bekamen, wenn sie auch 'in die Steine gingen', wie man die Aufräumarbeiten nannte. Das Angebot des Reeders nahmen sie an: zwei Tage in der Woche arbeiten, dafür bekamen sie für die ganze Woche einen Arbeitszeitnachweis. Ach ja, Lohn gab es natürlich nicht, aber trotzdem lohnte es sich offensichtlich auch für die Steuerleute, denn sie arbeiteten sehr gut. Anfangs 50 und später bis zu 600 Nieten wurden täglich geklopft. Durch den Bombentreffer und den Untergang hatten sich die meisten Nieten der ANNE gelockert und mußten kontrolliert werden. Der junge Reeder lernte nochmals dazu: Nietenklopfen, Spantenbiegen, Schweißen usw. Im Laufe des Jahres 1946 besserte sich die Situation, der Werkmeister der Werft motivierte seine Leute, es ging voran. Eines Tages mußten die Arbeiten unterbrochen werden, weil Anastasia aus den Staaten zu Besuch kam. Sie und ihr 'Hofstaat' hatten das alte Boot WASSERSCHUTZPOLIZEI 15 erworben und hofften das nun 'Kaiserliche Schiff' über 'abgefangene' Care-Pakete wieder aufmöbeln zu können. Sie war angeblich die einzige Überlebende

of metal from the ANNE and made them into heating stoves which they could cook on. Wehr found the answer when former classmates and officers contacted the new shipowner. Business on the black market was going well for them, but they also had to have employment notes, which were normally only available when they helped to clear rubble after bombing raids. So they accepted Wehr's offer to work two days a week in return for an employment note for the whole week, instead of wages. In spite of this, the arrangement obviously suited the seamen, as their work was good. Starting with 50 rivets, they eventually fitted 600 a day, as most of the ANNE's rivets had loosened after the bombing raid and sinking, so they all had to be checked. The young shipowner acquired new skills, which included riveting, frame bending and welding.

The situation improved in the course of 1946. The yard foreman managed to motivate his workers and things progressed. One day work came to a standstill because Anastasia arrived from the United States to visit the yard. She and her 'imperial household' had purchased the former river police patrol boat, the WASSERSCHUTZPOLIZEI 15, and were hoping to refurbish the 'imperial vessel' using CARE parcels. Allegedly she was the only survivor of the massacre of the Romanov Czar family by the Communists in 1918. Throughout her lifetime she fought in vain for recognition as the Czar's daughter. At the time she was still surrounded in splendour, though doubts had arisen. The Admiral of the Baltic Fleet arrived at the Wolkau yard in an old grey army uniform and announced to the workers that they were to brush themselves

des 1917 von den Kommunisten verübten Massakers an der Zarenfamilie Romanow. Um ihre Anerkennung als Zarentochter kämpfte sie jedoch zeitlebens vergeblich. Damals jedenfalls umgab sie noch Glanz, gleichwohl es die Zweifel schon gab. Der Admiral der Baltischen Flotte kam in einer alten feldgrauen Uniform auf die Wolkau Werft und sagte, 'Jungs bringt Euch und den Kahn auf Vordermann, morgen kommt die *Kaiserliche Hoheit'*. Hoheit kam und wurde allen Werft- und Reederei-Leuten vorgestellt. Herbert Wolkau begrüßte die Hoheit mit einem kurzen 'Tach, Fräulein Romanow!' Wehr hatte einen ehemaligen Offizier als Schiffsjungen eingestellt, der angesichts des vermeintlichen Glanzes garnicht wußte, wie er sich benehmen sollte. Wehr half ihm aus der Verlegenheit:
„Du hast keine Uniform an, also brauchst Du auch nicht strammzustehen."
Es ging weiterhin voran, Wolkau trieb im Sachsenwald Bäume auf, die das Material für die Lukenabdeckung hergaben. Einen Mast fand man nicht, ein Ladebaum wurde umgearbeitet. Man traf auch sonst auf nette Leute, die ohne Schnaps und Zigaretten halfen. Ehefrau Helga baute inzwischen in der Hausruine die Wohnung wieder auf, unten war nichts, oben war nichts, im ersten Stock wohnten Wehrs. Sie hatte Glück, daß ihr ein Maurermeister, Vater einer Freundin, half, die Steine zum neuen 'Heim' zusammenzufügen, die sie tagsüber freilegte.

and the ship up, as Her Imperial Highness was to arrive the next day. Her Highness duly arrived and was introduced to all the yard men and shipowner's staff. Herbert Wolkau greeted her with a curt 'Morning, Miss Romanov'. In his employment Wehr had a former officer as deckhand, who was so confused by the apparent grandeur that he had no idea how to behave. Wehr helped him overcome his embarrassment: *"You're not wearing uniform, so you don't have to stand to attention."* Things continued to progress. Wolkau managed to get trees from the nearby Sachsenwald which could be used for making the hatch covers. No mast could be found, so a derrick was converted instead. Others were kind enough to assist, even without payment in schnapps or cigarettes. Helga Wehr had meanwhile re-established their flat which had been bombed out. There was nothing on the ground floor, nothing above it. The Wehrs lived on the first floor, but were lucky: she collected bricks from the rubble which the father of a friend, a master bricklayer, used to rebuild their new home.

Finanzierung mit Fisch und Silberfüchsen

Einkommen hatte das junge Reeder-Ehepaar nicht, die fortschreitende Reparatur des Schiffs und die schon angeheuerte Besatzung kosteten Geld. Die am Schiff arbeitenden Leute entlohnte Wehr z. T. damit, indem er nachts am Altonaer Fischmarkt die Fische auflas, die beim Löschen aus den Körben fielen, sie räucherte und mit auf die Werft brachte. Natürlich langten die Fische nicht, zumal man Wehr trotz Offiziersuniform einige Male schnappte. Aus den Nordland-Seefahrtstagen besaß er noch eine mit Schaffell gefütterte Lederjacke. Auf eine solche Jacke waren viele Fischdampferleute scharf. Zwar hatte Wehr einen Schwager, der als Fischdampferkapitän zur See fuhr und die Jacke gern haben, aber nicht den geforderten Preis von sechs Fässern Heringe zahlen wollte. Ein Matrose des Dampfers ergriff die Chance sofort und bezahlte mit den Heringen. Oskar Wehr transportierte Faß für Faß vom Altonaer Fischereihafen nach Hause, wo er sich einen Räucherofen gebaut hatte. Es war viel Arbeit, die Fische zu verarbeiten und zu räuchern, aber nahrhafte Verpflegung außerhalb der Lebensmittelmarken war damals gefragt. Weil die Arbeiter außer essen auch rauchen wollten, bauten die Wehrs Tabak an. Gegenüber ihrem Wohnhaus befand sich ein Gartengrundstück, allerdings mit Bombentrichtern übersät.

„Mit einem Hilfsmann von Bord schütteten wir die Trichter mit Schutt zu, legten eine Schicht Erde darüber und bepflanzten den 'Garten' mit Tomaten, Salat und Tabakpflanzen. Helga mußte mit den geernteten Tabakblättern nach Bergedorf fahren, dort wurden sie geschnit-

Fish and furs

The young couple had no income as shipowners, but the repairs to the ship and the crew still had to be paid for. Wehr often paid the people working on his ship in kind. At night he would collect fish which had fallen off the baskets at the fish market in Altona, smoke it and take it to the yard. As payment the fish were not enough, of course, especially as Wehr had been caught collecting it more than once, even though he had been wearing his officer's uniform. From his time as sea in the Nordic regions Wehr still had a leather jacket lined with sheepskin, something fishing crews were keen to have. In fact Wehr had a brother-in-law who was skipper of a trawler. He wanted the jacket badly, but was not prepared to pay six barrels of herring for it, the asking price. A seaman from the same ship grabbed the chance and paid – in herring. From the fishing port in Altona Oskar Wehr took one barrel home at a time to be treated in the smokery he had built. He went to a lot of work preparing and smoking the fish, but over and above what one could get for ration cards, nourishing food was much in demand. The workers not only required food but cigarettes too, so the Wehrs planted tobacco on a garden plot opposite their house which was covered in craters from the bombs.

"Helped by a deckhand from the ship we filled in the craters with rubble, covered them with a layer of earth and planted tomatoes, lettuce and tobacco plants in our 'garden'. After picking, Helga had to take the tobacco leaves to Bergedorf, where they were cut and cured. The goods we delivered were first-class, which they had to be, as the shipyard

ten und fermentiert. Wir lieferten erstklassige Ware, was auch nötig war. Die Werftarbeiter bevorzugten englische Zigaretten, wenn es welche gab. Morgens kamen die Barkassen zur Erledigung kleinerer Reparaturen an die Werft, deren Eigner hatten Zigaretten und wir keine Arbeiter mehr. Ab Mittag wurde bei mir gearbeitet und deutscher Tabak geraucht, der schmeckte dann auch. Wie oft meine Frau nach Bergedorf zur 'Verarbeitung' gefahren ist, weiß ich nicht mehr, aber bei rund 250 Tabakpflanzen müssen es viele Fahrten gewesen sein.' Als alles schön blühte und gedieh auf 'unserem Grundstück', kam der Besitzer und wollte alles übernehmen. Wir einigten uns auf die Übergabe im nächsten Jahr und so konnten wir neben einem Jahr Schiff- und Häuserbau auch noch ein Jahr Landwirtschaft betreiben – was man nicht so alles macht, wenn Not am Mann ist."

Um die für das Schiff nötigen Materialien bezahlen zu können, verkaufte er nach und nach seine goldene Uhr, seine Leica, sein Fernglas, zwei Gläser, die für ihn Erinnerungen an den Kreuzer EMDEN darstellten. Ehefrau Helga trennte sich von ihrer Konfirmationsuhr sowie von einigen Teilen ihrer Aussteuerausstattung. Geld brachten auch die Silberfüchse aus Norwegen, die ihr Mann einst von der MAR DEL PLATA mitbrachte sowie Taschen, die man bei Leder-Schüler aus mitgebrachtem Leder anfertigen ließ und anschließend verkaufte. In jenen Zeiten war man sehr erfinderisch einerseits und sehr anspruchslos andererseits. Mit den Banken kam der junge Reeder und seinem alten Schiff nicht klar, also half er sich selbst. Zu den verläßlichen Besatzungsmitgliedern gehörte der Matrose Herbert Nissen. Bis zur Steuermannschule fuhr er bei Wehr und wurde dann sehr schnell Kapitän, er heiratete die Tochter von

Diese Aufnahme von Oskar Wehr entstand 1944.
Oskar Wehr in 1944.

workers preferred English cigarettes if they could get them. In the morning launches would arrive at the shipyard with men to carry out smaller repairs. Their owners had cigarettes, so we lost our workers to them. From noon on they worked for me, smoking German tobacco, which they enjoyed as well. I can't remember how often my wife went to Bergedorf to have the tobacco treated, but with around 250 plants, she must have made quite a few trips. Once everything on 'our' plot was in full boom and flourishing, the owner appeared and wanted to take it over again. We agreed to hand it over the following year, so for one whole year we were farmers as well as being in the shipping and house-building business. You become very enterprising when times are bad."

To pay for the materials he needed for his ship, Oskar Wehr had to sell his gold watch, his Leica camera, his binoculars, and two glasses which had been souvenirs from the EMDEN, the cruiser he had sailed on. Helga Wehr parted with the watch she had received

Herbert Nissen am Steuer der ANNE.
Herbert Nissen at the wheel of the ANNE.

Klaus Nagel aus Drochtersen. Er ging mit Frau und Kind mit der BERTHA KIENASS, einer zum Kümo umgebauten Korvette, um den Monatswechsel Januar/Februar 1962 vor Texel unter. Das Schiff war auf eine Mine gelaufen

Im September 1947 kam die ANNE in Fahrt. Die Versicherungsgilde 'Einigkeit Drochtersen' nahm den Neuling sofort auf, woran sich Kapitän Wehr heute noch gern erinnert, denn das war durchaus keine Selbstverständlichkeit. Er fand dort viele Freunde. Wegen der sehr eingeschränkten Seefahrtsmöglichkeiten startete ANNE in der Fahrt auf den westdeutschen Kanälen. Dortmund-Ems-Kanal, Weser-Datteln-Kanal, Rhein-Herne-Kanal usw. waren die Wasserstraßen, auf denen das kleine Schiff fuhr. Schiffseigner Oskar Wehr hatte sich, seitdem sein Plan, Küstenschiffer zu werden, feststand, immer von erfahrenen Küstenschiffern beraten lassen, vor allem von den Haren/Emsern, die in der Kanal- und Rheinfahrt zu Hause waren und noch sind. So konnte ANNE nicht nur unter Motor, Segel oder beidem fahren, der Mast war

for her confirmation and some of the things she had received for her dowry. Silver fox furs from Norway also brought in money. These her husband had brought home with him on the MAR DEL PLATA. They also sold bags which they had made from leather he had brought with him, which they took to Leder-Schüler, the leather shop, to be made up, then sold. In those days one had to use one's ingenuity, but on the other hand people were more unassuming. The young shipowner and his old ship had problems with the bank, so Wehr had to rely on his own devices.

One of the reliable members of the crew was the seaman Herbert Nissen. He sailed with Wehr until going to nautical college, then was quickly promoted to master when he returned to sea. He married Klaus Nagel's daughter from Drochtersen. He, his wife and child all lost their lives in January or early February 1962, when the BERTHA KIENASS, a corvette which had been converted into a coaster, hit a mine off Texel.

The ANNE was taken into commission in September 1947. The insurance guild 'Einigkeit Drochtersen' admitted the newcomer without hesitation. Looking back Captain Wehr was grateful for this, as members were not accepted as a matter of course. He made many friends in Drochtersen. As shipping was extremely restricted at the time, the ANNE started her commercial life on West German canals: the Dortmund-Ems Kanal, the Weser-Datteln Kanal and the Rhine-Herne Kanal were all home waters for the coaster. Ever since deciding to become a coastal skipper Oskar Wehr had heeded the advice of experienced skippers, mainly from the Haren-Ems region, who knew both the Rhine and canal

klappbar und das Ruderhaus demontierbar. Zur Besatzung gehörte nicht nur Ehefrau Helga, sondern auch Sohn Jürgen, der im Juni 1947 geboren und ebenso wie seine Schwester Marianne auf den Schiffen des Vaters groß wurde. Kohle war eine der häufigsten Ladungen. Eine solche Reise führte ANNE mit Kohle zu einer Bunkerstation eben außerhalb des Nord-Ostsee-Kanals. Der Laderaum ließ sich mit Greifern relativ schnell löschen, aber knapp 30 Tonnen lagen achtern unter dem Roof, dem Aufbau, und mußten von Hand herausgeschaufelt werden. Der Arbeiter der Bunkerstation fluchte, sah dann aber in der Kombüse eine blaue Dose mit dänischer Butter stehen. Ein Gespräch zwischen Arbeiter und Schiffer begann, eine Lösung für das Problem der schwer zugänglichen 30 Tonnen Kohle wurde gefunden. Der Arbeiter ging mit dänischer Dosenbutter, Whisky und 1000 Mark von Bord, organisierte die nächtliche Durchfahrt der ANNE in den Kanal (bei Tageslicht durfte sie mit ihrem Ladungsrest schließlich nicht mehr an der Pier liegen) und Schiffer Wehr steuerte die Oste an, die er bestens kannte. Dort brauchte er nicht lange zu warten, bis Bauern mit ihren Fuhrwerken ankamen, weil sich herumgesprochen hatte, daß einige Tonnen Kohle zu haben waren. Bargeld floß nicht. Drei Tage später als geplant lief ANNE den Hamburger Hafen an, im Laderaum Hammel-, Rindfleisch, Hühner, Speck und Eier. Das Konservieren und Verhökern der wertvollen Fracht nahm zwar viele Tage und Nächte in Anspruch, es hatte sich jedoch gelohnt. Solche 'Geschäfte' (verjährt!) bildeten jedoch die absolute Ausnahme.

Gleich nach der Währungsreform lag das Schiff sechs Wochen still, sein Kapitän Wehr lag mit

ANNE (vorn) schleppt das Schiff eines Kollegen.
The ANNE (foreground) towing a colleague's ship.

trade inside out. The ANNE was able to sail under engine power, under sail alone or both together; she had a collapsible mast and her wheelhouse was detachable. Helga Wehr was not the only member of the crew. Their son Jürgen had been born in June 1947. He and his sister Marianne both grew up on their father's ships. Coal was one of the cargoes they carried most frequently. On one such trip the ANNE was heading for a bunkering station just off the Kiel Canal. The main hold could be discharged comparatively quickly by grab but there were still 30 tonnes of coal under the 'roof,' which had to be shovelled by hand. The worker at the bunkering station cursed his lot until he discovered a blue tin with Danish butter in the galley. A discussion was started between the workman and the skipper until they found a solution to the problem. The man left the ship with the tin of Danish butter, some whisky and 1,000 Marks. He also arranged a night passage for the ANNE through the canal (as the ship was not

Typhus im Krankenhaus. Mit Hilfe eines Kriegskameraden ihres Mannes brachte Helga Wehr das Schiff nach Hamburg zum Löschen, und um die 40 DM Kopfgeld, die jeder Bundesbürger zur Währungsreform bekam, im Heimatort abzuholen.

Oskar Wehr zog es immer vor, sich eigene Nischen zu suchen, statt im großen Durchschnittsstrom der anderen mitzufahren. Er machte das Rheinpatent und steuerte mit der ANNE Destinationen auf dem Niederrhein an, wobei das Fahren zu Berg Zeit und Nerven kostet. ANNE kam gegen den Strom kaum an und brauchte beladen für die rund 95 Stromkilometer von Duisburg nach Köln runde zwei Tage. In Ballast machte ANNE mehr Fahrt und hatte einmal sogar Andernach als Ziel. Das Schiff fuhr einige Zeit für Lehnkering Stückgut von vielen Rheinhäfen in die Nordsee. Es gab zwischen 14 und 15 DM für die Tonne Stückgut, das sich aus Chemikalien und Eisenprodukten zusammensetzte. Eine volle Ladung bestand aus vielen Partien, die an mehreren Ladeplätzen eingesammelt werden mußten.

„Es klappte immer gut, ich konnte ankommen wann ich wollte, ich bekam gleich meine Ladungspartie und konnte weiterfahren. Bei gutem Wetter ging es bei Terschelling in die Nordsee, bei schlechtem Wetter über die niederländischen Kanäle in die Emsmündung."
Eine Reise folgte der anderen.
„Wir sind bis zur totalen Erschöpfung gefahren".
Es wurde gearbeitet und gespart. Reparaturen an der betagten ANNE wurden alle selbst ausgeführt. Der Rumpf wurde bei Ebbe im Watt gestrichen und selbst Arbeiten an der Schraube und am Ruder führte der schwimm- und

allowed to stay tied up at the pier with the remaining cargo on board). Skipper Wehr then headed for the Oste, which he knew like the back of his hand. In a short time farmers began to arrive with their horse-drawn carts, as the news had got around that there was coal to be had. No cash was exchanged, but the ANNE arrived in Hamburg three days later than planned, with mutton, beef, chicken, bacon and eggs in her hold. It took a few days and nights to bottle and sell such valuable cargo, but it was worth every minute. 'Business' of that kind (invalidated by now, of course) was definitely the exception.

Following the currency reform the ship lay idle for six weeks as Captain Wehr was in hospital with typhoid fever. Assisted by a wartime comrade of her husband's, Helga Wehr took the ship to Hamburg to be discharged, so that she could collect the 40 Deutschmarks every West German citizen was entitled to in her home town, when the currency was changed.

Oskar Wehr had always preferred to cut a niche for himself rather than follow the general crowd. He got his Rhine Captain's licence and called in at ports on the Lower Rhine with the ANNE, even though trips upriver proved time-consuming and nerve-wracking. The ANNE hardly made any way at all going upstream and fully-loaded took about two days to cover the 95 kilometres of river between Duisburg and Cologne. In ballast she was faster and even went as far as Andernach on one trip. For a time the ship carried general cargo for Lehnkering from various Rhine to North Sea ports. One tonne of general cargo would bring in DM 14 to DM 15 and consisted of chemicals and steel products. A full cargo

ANNE unter Segel gut abgeladen auf See.
ANNE under sails at sea, down to her marks.

Jürgen und Marianne Wehr an Bord der ANNE.
Jürgen and Marianne Wehr on board the ANNE.

was made up of several lots which had to be collected at several loading points. "Things always went well. No matter what time I arrived I always got my allotted cargo and could set off again. If the weather was good we entered the North Sea near Terschelling, but if it was bad, we used the Dutch canals to the mouth of the River Ems." *One trip followed the next, without a break.* "We kept going till we dropped from exhaustion."

They worked hard and saved money. They carried out all repairs on the ageing ANNE themselves. They painted the hull when the tide was out on the mud-flats. Being an experienced swimmer and diver, the owner repaired the propeller and rudder himself too. Once Wehr manoeuvred his ship under a bridge in Hamburg – the Trostbrücke – where

taucherprobte Eigner selbst. Einmal manövrierte Wehr sein Schiff unter die Hamburger Trostbrücke und vertäute es gut. Um einen Pfeiler legten die Helfer eine Talje und befestigten an den Enden das Ruder. Mit der einsetzenden Ebbe sackte das Schiff weg, bis zum nächsten Hochwasser mußte die Reparatur beendet sein.

„Ich habe in den neun Jahren mit der ANNE soviel körperlich gearbeitet wie vorher und hinterher nie wieder, aber ich habe auch Geld verdient", erinnert sich der Reeder heute, und daß er eines nie geschafft hat, nämlich mit ANNE einmal westwärts 'außenrum' zu fahren, d. h. vor den ost- und westfriesischen Nordseeinseln bis nach Holland, immer war das Wetter schlecht. Einmal hatte Kapitän Wehr 24 Stunden Norderney querab, es ging einfach nicht weiter, so sehr steamte es gegenan. Auf einer anderen Reise kam das Schiff gar nicht erst an den osfriesischen Inseln vorbei. Kapitän Wehr entschloß sich, die Inseln 'binnenwärts zu nehmen' und ging in Wilhelmshaven in den Ems-Jade-Kanal, der über Aurich nach Emden führt. Das leere Schiff kam auch gut voran, bis bei Schirum eine besonders niedrige Brücke dem Schiff trotz abmontierten Ruderhauses und geklappter Masten die Durchfahrt verwehrte. Oskar Wehr dachte nach, zurück wollte er nicht (er hätte eine lange Strecke rückwärts fahren müssen), und in Emden wartete Ladung auf ihn. Also flutete er den leeren Laderaum, das Schiff tauchte tiefer ein und kam unter der Brücke durch. Die Findigkeit lohnte sich jedoch nicht. Als das Schiff endlich in Emden ankam, war die Ladung annulliert, und durch das Wasser im Raum waren alle Bugdielen hochgekommen und mußten mit erheblichem Arbeitsaufwand repariert werden.

he tied her up safely. His men fastened a pulley to one of the pillars and secured the rudder to it. The ship was lowered with the ebb-tide. Repairs had to be finished by the time the next tide came in.

"In the nine years I was on the ANNE I did more manual labour than I'd ever done before or did after, but I earned money," was how the shipowner recalled it. *He also remembers that he had never been able to sail west with the ANNE 'round' the Netherlands to Holland, north of the Friesian islands, as the weather had always been too bad. On one trip Captain Wehr battled against headwinds for 24 hours off the island of Norderney. There was just no headway to be made. Another time the ship was unable to pass the East Friesian islands, so Wehr took the inland waterway route instead, going through the Ems-Jade Canal from Wilhelmshaven, which runs to Emden via Aurich. The empty vessel made good progress until they came to a particularly low bridge near Schirum. Even with the mast lowered and wheelhouse dismantled, it was impossible to pass under it. Oskar Wehr thought about it: he did not want to go back (as he had already covered a good distance) and had cargo waiting for him in Emden. So he flooded the empty hold to lower the ship and they managed to negotiate the bridge. Resourceful as this was, the idea did not pay off. By the time the ship arrived in Emden the cargo had been cancelled and all the floorboarding in the bow of the hold had warped due to the water. The ship had to be repaired at great expense.*

Einfallsreichtum bei zu kurzen Schleusen

Dann entdeckten ANNE und ihr Reeder den Vänern- und den Vätternsee in Schweden. Beide waren durch den von 1810 bis 1832 von Baltazar von Platen gebauten Göta-Kanal erreichbar. ANNE paßte gerade in die 22 Schleusen, die nur Schiffe von 30 m Länge, sieben Meter Breite und 2,8 m Tiefgang aufnahmen. Anfang der fünfziger Jahre waren die beiden größten schwedischen Seen für deutsche Schiffe noch relativ unbekannt, mit dem späteren Ausbau des Trollhättan-Kanals gelangten auch größere Schiffe in den Vänernsee. Auf der Leerfahrt in den See gab es keine Probleme, der überfallende Klipperbug ragte weit über den Drempel der Schleuse, von denen man nicht wenige selbst bedienen mußte. Aber auf der Rückreise wurde es dann eng, ANNE war – mit Ladung wesentlich tiefer eingetaucht – zu lang für die Schleuse. 'Det gör inte' sagte der schwedische Schleusenmeister und schlug eine kostspielige Prozedur vor: ANNE mit Schleppern wieder (rückwärts) in den Vetter-See ziehen, dann drehen und über Södertälje (im Osten Schwedens) raus in die See. Das war dem Reeder zu langwierig und zu teuer. Er baute das Ruder ab (und wieder an – und das viele Male) und sein Schiff hatte auch beladen wieder Schleusenmaß. Auf der Steuermannsschule hatte er gelernt, die komplizierten Stabilitätsrechnungen, z. B. für Holz, selbst vorzunehmen. So ging er in die Holzfahrt, die damals für nahezu alle Kümogrößen ein lukratives Betätigungsgebiet darstellte. 54 Standards konnte sein kleines Schiff laden, die Sicht vom Ruderhaus nach vorn war dann wesentlich ein-

Ingenuity in short locks

The ANNE and her owner eventually discovered the Vänern and Vättern Lakes in Sweden. Access to both was via the Göta Canal, which had been built between 1810 and 1832 by Baltazar von Platen. The ANNE just fit in to the twenty-two locks, which took ships of up to 30 metres long, seven metres wide and with a draft of 2.80 metres. In the early fifties the two lakes – Sweden's largest – were still relatively unknown to German shipping. Bigger ships were only able to sail into Lake Vänern after the Trollhättan Canal had been built. When empty, sailing into the Lake presented no problems, as the clipper-type bow of the ship protruded well clear of the sill of the lock. Many locks still had to be operated manually by the crew. Things were tighter on the return trip. With cargo, the draft of the ANNE was deeper and she was too long for the lock. 'Det gor inte,' said the Swedish lockmaster, suggesting a risky procedure. This was to tow the ANNE (backwards) into Lake Vättern, turn her round and take her out to sea via Södertälje in East Sweden. The owner considered this prospect too time-consuming and too expensive. So he dismantled the rudder (putting it back repeatedly as well) and his ship fit into the lock even with cargo on board. At college he had been taught how to do complicated stability calculations – for cargoes of timber, for instance. This lead him to go into the timber trade, a remunerative proposition at the time for coasters of almost every size. His ship was able to take 54 standards of timber, which meant the view from the wheelhouse was comparatively restricted. On one trip to Bremen the ANNE's cargo was stacked so high that if a storm were

geschränkt. Auf einer Reise nach Bremen war ANNE so hoch beladen, daß Kapitän Wehr bei Sturm sie weder beim Zoll noch auf der Weser beidrehen konnte, sie wäre umgekippt.

„Was nicht sein durfte kam: Sturm und das nicht zu knapp!"

'De Lüüd' an Land zeigten Verständnis, ganz vorsichtig lief das Schiff den Löschplatz in Bremen an, und erleichtert war ihr Eigner erst, als die ersten Hieven an Land waren.

'So zwischendurch' machte Oskar Wehr 1951 das Patent A 6, womit er nun Kapitän auf Großer Fahrt war. Während der Schulzeit fuhr Setzschiffer Flunghusen die ANNE. Nun mit einem großen Patent ausgerüstet, strebte Wehr auch nach einem größeren Schiff. Weil das schwierig war, ließ er ANNE 1952 verlängern. Die 20.000 DM, die Herbert Wolkau für die Sechs-Meter-Sektion haben wollte, waren ihm zuviel, und so überraschte er Grube in Warwisch mit dem Angebot, sie dürften ihm das Schiff um sechs Meter verlängern. Er bot freiwillig 1000 DM pro laufenden Meter, Basis 'all in'. Das akzeptierte die Werft, bereute es aber später, weil die Verlängerung ziemlich kompliziert und damit kein Geschäft war. Grube lernte die Vorschriften des Germanischen Lloyd kennen, und anschließend hatte Wehr ein Schiff, das trotz der geringen Geschwindigkeit wirtschaftlicher war als vorher. Bei neun Mark und 100 Tonnen Kohle vom Ruhrgebiet zur Elbe war ein großer Überschuß nicht möglich. Nach der Verlängerung lief es besser, weil die Wirtschaft zunehmend in Schwung kam, an Holz konnten etwa 15 Standards mehr als zuvor geladen werden. Immerhin stand der junge Eigner besser da als seine angestellten Kapitäns-Kollegen, die damals in der Nord-Ostsee-Fahrt etwa 450 DM und in der Großen Fahrt 600 DM verdienten.

to come up, Wehr would have been unable to heave to, either for Customs or at the River Weser. His ship would have capsized. *"A storm did come up – and what a storm, too."* The people ashore realised what was happening as the ship inched into her berth in Bremen, ready for discharging. Her owner breathed a sigh of relief when the first lots had been lifted. 'In between' Oskar Wehr prepared for his ocean-going Master's license examination, and in 1951 passed. While he was studying, his job on the ANNE was taken over by a relief skipper called Flunghusen. With his new license Wehr started looking for a bigger ship. As that proved difficult, he had the ANNE lengthened in 1952. Wehr considered the DM 20,000 Herbert Wolkau was asking for the new 6-metre midship section excessive. So he sprang at the proposition from the Grube yard at Warwisch to fit a 6-metre section into his ship at an all-in price of DM 1,000 per (running) metre. The shipyard accepted. But they were to regret their decision later, because it turned out to be a complicated job, one which did not pay them well. In the process Grube learned all about Germanischer Lloyd's stipulations. By the time Wehr took redelivery he had a much more profitable vessel than before, in spite of her low speed. At freight rates of nine Deutschmarks and a cargo of 100 tonnes of coal from the Ruhr to the Elbe, profit margins were low. Extending the ship had helped, as the ship could now carry 15 standards of timber more, and the economy was starting to pick up. At any rate the young shipowner was doing better than his colleagues who were employed as masters and were only earning about DM 450 in short-sea trading areas and DM 600 on ocean-going vessels.

Nach der Verlängerung war die ANNE mit ihren knapp 160 Ladetonnen ein interessantes Schiff geworden. Ab 160 Tonnen Ladung mußte man z. B. in dänischen Häfen, die oft angelaufen wurden, Stauereiarbeiter annehmen, bis 159 Tonnen lag die Entscheidung beim Kapitän. Die Umschlagarbeiten waren mit der eigenen Besatzung und tatkräftiger Hilfe des Kapitäns natürlich billiger zu bewerkstelligen als mit einer kompletten Stauerei-Gang. Je nach Ladung nahm Kapitän Wehr einen Mann von Land an, die Liegezeit war schließlich auch ein zu berücksichtigender Aspekt.

Das am 14. August 1952 in Kraft getretene Lastenausgleichsgesetz hatte zum Inhalt, die Schäden und Verluste eines Teils des deutschen Volkes infolge von Vertreibungen und Zerstörungen der Kriegs- und Nachkriegszeit sowie besondere Härten, die durch die Währungs-

Her extension had made the ANNE a more interesting ship, as she could now carry nearly 160 tonnes of cargo. She often called at Danish ports, where stevedores were compulsory for cargoes over 160 tonnes. With a cargo up to 159 tonnes the decision to take on stevedores or not was left to the master. Loading and discharging cargo was of course cheaper if crew labour was used – actively supported by the master – rather than employing a full gang of stevedores. Depending on the cargo, Captain Wehr would take on one man from shore, as time in port was also a factor which had to be considered.

On 14th August 1952 a new German law came into force designed to balance out losses suffered by some of the population due to being expelled from and having suffered destruction to their property during and after the

ANNE nach der Verlängerung *ANNE after lengthening.*

reform entstanden waren, auszugleichen. Oskar Wehr hatte nichts im Osten verloren, aber im Westen ein Schiff mit einem Gesamtaufwand von 270.000 Mark vor der Währungsreform in Fahrt gesetzt und somit Eigentum geschaffen. Daß dies nur mit erheblichen Eigenaufwand und Verzicht auf fast alles Private geschehen konnte, blieb unberücksichtigt. Das Schiff hatte zwar einiges an Geld aufgefahren und Kredite getilgt, war aber 1952 nur etwa 40.000 DM wert. Basierend auf dem Reparaturbetrag von 1947 hatte Oskar Wehr einen hohen Lastenausgleich zu zahlen, einen Betrag, der seine finanziellen Möglichkeiten überforderte. Die Forderung bestand und Oskar Wehr mußte sehen, wie er sie abtragen konnte.

war, and to compensate for special hardship as a result of the currency reform. Oskar Wehr had suffered no losses in the East but, with a total investment of 270,000 Marks, had taken a ship into commission in West Germany prior to the currency reform, which constituted property. No allowance was made for the fact that he had achieved this by substantial personal effort, expenditure and sacrifice. The ship had subsequently earned money to repay the credit but was only worth about DM 40,000 in 1952. On the basis of the Reparation Agreement of 1947 Oskar Wehr had a considerable amount to pay. It was more than he could afford. The claim was still there however, and Oskar Wehr had to find a way to pay it.

Dieses Dockbild von HELGA WEHR zeigt deutlich den Fischdampferkiel.

HELGA WEHR in drydock. Note her trawler keel.

Ein größeres Schiff mit scharfem Kiel

Mit einem größeren Schiff war das natürlich eher möglich. Heinrich Peill, ein bekannter Busunternehmer, der sein Unternehmen an die Post verkaufte, hatte sich von der Werft Gebr. Wandmaker & Sohn an der Hamburger Süderelbe zwischen den Elbbrücken einen Fischdampfer in ein modernes Küstenmotorschiff umbauen lassen. Aus dem 1919 von Joh. C. Tecklenborg gebauten 249 BRT-Fischdampfer LUDWIG SANDERS war von Juli 1952 bis April 1953 das 350 BRT-Küstenmotorschiff DÖRTE entstanden. Peill fuhr auf seinem Schiff allerdings 'big ship style', Kapitän, Steuermann, Maschinist, Koch und fünf Mann an Deck, kam so nicht zurecht und wollte das Schiff verkaufen. *„Ich besichtigte das Schiff und schlug die Hände überm Kopf zusammen, so sah der Dampfer aus. Aber dann sagte ich mir, besser als dein Wrack aus der Tiefe ist* DÖRTE *auf alle Fälle."*
Die Finanzierung gestaltete sich schwierig. Wiederaufbaudarlehen und ähnliches bekam die Hamburger Reederei Wehr nicht. 100.000 DM hatte Wehr, 420.000 DM forderte Heinrich Peill, das waren schon 60.000 DM weniger, als nur der reine Umbau gekostet hatte. Der erste Kreditantrag Wehrs an seine Hamburger Sparkasse wurde glatt abgelehnt, für ein knapp 35 Jahre altes Schiff wollte man keine 70 Prozent Darlehen geben. Beim zweiten Antrag ließ der Banker dann verlauten, „wenn sie denn wenigstens einen Bürgen hätten!" Ehe Wehr nachdenken konnte, wer denn nun wohl dafür in Frage käme, stand Direktor Schütt von der Hamburger Sparkasse auf, mit dem er all die Jahre gut zusammen gearbeitet hatte und sagte:

Larger ship – deeper keel

With a larger ship repayment could, of course, be effected more quickly. Heinrich Peill, a well-known owner of a bus service, had sold the business to the Post and with the proceeds had a trawler converted into a modern coaster at the Wandmaker & Sohn shipyard, which was located between the bridges crossing the south arm of the River Elbe. The 249 GRT trawler LUDWIG SANDERS, which had been built by Joh. C. Tecklenborg in 1919, then became the 350 GRT coaster DÖRTE. Carrying out the conversion took from July 1952 to April 1953. Peill's crewing standards were still old-fashioned (Master, Second Mate, Engineer, Cook and five hands on deck), which did not make ends meet. He was therefore looking for a buyer. *"I looked around the ship and found it in appalling condition. But then the* DÖRTE *was still better than the wreck I'd raised from the depths."*
Financing it proved hard. Wehr did not qualify for reconstruction loans or similar credit. He had DM 100,000 and Peill was asking DM 420,000 – DM 60,000 less than conversion alone would have cost. Wehr's first application for credit at the Hamburger Sparkasse (the Hamburg savings bank) was turned down, as the bank refused to grant a 70% loan for a 35-year-old ship. On his next attempt Wehr was told *"if you had someone who could guarantee the money…"* Before Wehr could think of a likely candidate, Schütt, who was a director of the Hamburger Sparkasse and who had been extremely co-operative with Wehr over the years, got up and said: *"I know Mr Wehr is a*

„Ich habe Herrn Wehr als ordentlichen Kaufmann kennnengelernt, ich bürge für ihn." Der Kreditausschuß genehmigte das Darlehen, Direktor Schütt mußte seine Bürgschaft nie erfüllen. Wehr zahlte pünktlich ab.

Auf der ersten Reise unter seinem Kommando lernte er kennen, was es heißt, einen ehemaligen Fischdampfer zu fahren. Er hätte drehen müssen, um beim Zoll anzulegen, aber die Elbe war einfach nicht breit genug. Der mit einem scharfen Kiel gebaute Frachter ließ sich im Fahrwasserstrom nicht drehen, rückwärts kam er bei den staunenden Zöllnern an. Wo immer eine Strömung stand, waren größere Drehungen schwierig, aber die HELGA WEHR, wie das neue Schiff nun hieß, war in ihrem Fahrtgebiet bald überall bekannt, einschließlich ihrer kleinen Macken. Den britischen Lotsen brauchte man nur zu sagen, 'she has been a trawler', dann konnten sie mit dem Schiff gut umgehen.

Leider hatte Kapitän Wehr bereits auf der dritten Reise mit seiner HELGA WEHR Pech. Bei Dragör lief er auf das Wrack des dort am 29. Oktober 1954 nach einer Kollision gesunkenen Dampfers NAVEN (1021 BRT/1917), weil die gesetzte Wracktonne der Ansteuerungstonne Dragör zum Verwechseln ähnlich sah. Der Fischdampferkiel verhinderte Schlimmeres, das Seeamt sah die Ursachen in einer Verkettung unvorhergesehener Umstände. Zwar versuchten Kapitän und Besatzung, das Schiff mit eigener Kraft vom Wrack herunterzubekommen, aber auch das Überbordwerfen von Ladung nützte nichts. Als es auf 8/9 Windstärken aufbriste, wurde es ungemütlich. Ein Berger zog das Schiff runter, und nach den üblichen Untersuchungen und Verklarungen kam das Schiff nach Hamburg und reparierte hier. Dar-

HELGA WEHR (1)

reputable businessman. I will guarantee for him personally." The credit committee agreed to the loan and Schütt never had to pay a thing. Wehr paid off the loan punctually.

On the new ship's first trip under Wehr's command he realized just what running a former trawler entailed. The ship was required to land at the Customs quay for inspection, but the Elbe was just not wide enough for her. The freighter with its deep keel was unable to turn

über war insbesondere die Bank glücklich: „Ein Glück, daß Sie hier sind, regen Sie sich nicht auf, das Schiff kriegen wir schon repariert, hier vor allem billiger als in Schweden, wo der Germanische Lloyd erst eine Reparatur wünschte!" Sie waren ob Wehrs Umsicht dankbar.

„Da meine Versicherungsscheine von vier Gilden ausgestellt war – je 100.000 DM – zeigte ich dem Besichtiger nur eine Summe. Dadurch

about in the river so, to the amazement of the Customs officials, the ship landed alongside in reverse. Making wide turns whenever there was a current proved problematic. However it did not take long for the HELGA WEHR (the new name of the ship) to become well known in her trading area, including her quirks. The British pilots only needed to know that she had been a trawler and they knew how to handle her.

kostete die Versicherung die Bergung nur 25 Prozent!"

Anschließend beschäftigte Oskar Wehr sein Schiff in der Holzfahrt, 170, wenn es sehr gut ging, auch 172 Standards Holz konnte das Schiff laden, lag dann allerdings auch an der absoluten Belastungsgrenze. Als Löschhäfen hatte er sich vor allem Häfen an der britischen Westküste ausgesucht, solche, die die Eigner von Plattbodenschiffen verschmähten, weil die Schadengefahr groß war. Auch nach Irland führten viele Reisen. Wenn doppelt so hohe Raten nach britischen Westküstenplätzen oder nach Nantes, Bordeaux und anderen französischen Häfen gezahlt wurden als zur englischen Ostküste, akzeptierte Wehr. Viel Konkurrenz gab es nicht. Lagen die Raten niedriger, fuhr auch HELGA WEHR zur Ostküste. Der scharfe Fischdampferkiel, der zwar beim Trockenfallen bei Ebbe durch die Kentergefahr nicht günstig war, hatte sich aber beim Ballastschiff bewährt, da er die Wellen 'schnitt'. Er hatte sich bezahlt gemacht. Innerhalb von zwei Jahren konnte der restliche Kaufpreis bezahlt werden, der Lastenausgleich und Steuerforderungen wurden beglichen. Es ging aufwärts. Zwar verabschiedete sich mal hier eine Pumpe und dort erlitt ein Ventil einen Schaden, aber etliches reparierte und wartete die Besatzung selbst. Auch eine vom Hersteller auf 54.000 DM veranschlagte Maschinenüberholung ließ sich mit Einfallsreichtum auf 4000 DM reduzieren. Der Eigner forderte nämlich einen Monteur an, der auf Stundenbasis arbeitete und die Besatzung zur Wartung anleitete. Das war viel billiger als alles vom Maschinenhersteller machen zu lassen. Das Schiff verdiente gutes Geld. Allein 1955 hatte die HELGA WEHR 450.000 DM aufgefahren, das war Rekord für diese Schiffsgröße.

Unfortunately bad luck struck on Captain Wehr's third trip with the HELGA WEHR. Having mistaken the wreck buoy of the S/S NAVEN (1021 GRT/1917), which had sunk in a collision on 29th October 1954, for the Dragör approach buoy, he hit the wreck. The keel of the ex-trawler prevented worse damage and the court decision pronounced by the Maritime Court was that the accident had been caused by a series of unforeseen circumstances. Both Master and crew tried to free the ship from the wreck under her own power but failed, even after jettisoning cargo. When a force 8 to 9 wind blew up things got unpleasant and the HELGA WEHR was towed off the wreck by a salvage tug. After the usual surveys and sea protests she went back to Hamburg for repairs. This pleased the bank: *"A good thing you came back. Don't worry. We'll get repairs done much more cheaply here than in Sweden, which is where Germanischer Lloyd wanted the work done."* The bankers appreciated Wehr's insight. *"As my insurance certificates had been issued by four guilds, each for DM 100,000, I only showed the surveyor one. This meant salvage for the insurance company only amounted to 25%."*

After the incident the ship was used for timber trading. She could take 170 standards of wood – and even 172 if things went well, but that was her absolute maximum. The discharging ports Wehr had chosen to use were on the west coast of Britain, mainly those scoffed at by flat-bottom boat owners due to the high risk of damage. He also called at Irish ports frequently. Even if rates there or at French ports such as Nantes, Bordeaux were twice those on the east coast of England, there was virtually no competition. When the rates were lower the

Nun ist das Werk zu End'gebracht,
viel Hände schafften Tag und Nacht,
die schwerste Arbeit ward getan,
genau nach des Erbauers Plan.

Gemeinsam wirkten Kopf und Hand
damit dies stolze Schiff entstand,
das jetzt zum Stapellauf bereit
und von den Helgen nun befreit
sich seinem Element vertraut
zum Stolze aller, die's gebaut.

Du Schiff, das meinen Namen hat,
Dir "Jürgen Wehr" wünsch ich immer gute Fahrt,
sei stark im Sturm, hab allzeit Glück,
kehr in die Heimat heil zurück!

Der Taufspruch für JÜRGEN WEHR (1).
Unten JÜRGEN WEHR (1) in der Ablieferungsversion.

(above:) The naming poem for mv JÜRGEN WEHR (1).
(below:) mv JÜRGEN WEHR (1) as delivered from the builders.

HELGA WEHR would also go to east coast ports in the UK. The ship's deep trawler keel was a drawback on an ebb tide, when the ship fell dry and there was danger of her capsizing, but in ballast the keel fairly cut through the waves. The purchase had paid off. Within two years Wehr had paid the remainder of the purchase price, balanced out his debts and paid his taxes. Things were looking up. There would be the odd breakdown – a pump or valve, for instance – but the crew carried out most of the repairs and maintenance themselves. Wehr even managed to reduce the price for an engine overhaul (originally estimated at DM 54,000) to DM 4,000 by using his imagination. He employed his own engineer, who was paid by the hour and instructed the crew in servicing the engine. This proved much cheaper than having the engine overhauled by the manufacturer. The ship was earning well. In 1955 her total earnings amounted to DM 450,000, a record for a ship of her size.

1957 lieferte Sietas den ersten Neubau

Im Sommer 1955 konnte Oskar Wehr sich seinen Traum erfüllen, er bestellte bei Johann Jacob Sietas in Neuenfelde einen Neubau. Die vom Land Hamburg zu stellende Landesbürgschaft hatte er innerhalb von 14 Tagen, worauf Oskar Wehr sehr stolz war, weil er sein neues Schiff nun schnell haben wollte. Sietas gratulierte ihm zwar zur schnellen Sicherstellung der Finanzierung, sagte aber, das hätten die anderen Eigner auch hinbekommen. Sietas versicherte, daß er 18 Monate Lieferzeit benötigte. Peter Döhle, damals noch Angestellter in Diensten der Firma Robert Bornhofen KG, hatte mehrere Eigner, die diesen Schiffstyp eines 424-BRT-Singledecker bauen ließen und war an weiteren Schiffen dieses Typs zur Erfüllung seiner Kontrakte interessiert. Er versprach seine Einflußnahme auf eine schnellere Lieferzeit, während Wehrs Hausmakler Bauer & Hausschildt KG ihm prophezeihte, daß er das Schiff 'nie' bekäme. Dem nicht ausgesprochenen Zusatz, in der Lieferzeit, die Döhle ihm versprach, lag dann eine Mißdeutung zugrunde. Da hatte Wehr durch Vermittlung eines MaK-Vertreters schon zu Döhle ans Kontor zu Bornhofen gewechselt, weil dieser ihm ebenfalls 450.000 DM Frachtaufkommen brutto im Jahr versprach, zudem in Bälde einen Neubau. Aber das Schiff kam nicht so schnell in Fahrt wie von Döhle versprochen. Am 14. November 1957 übernahm Oskar Wehr den nach seinem Sohn benannten Küstenmotorschiffsneubau JÜRGEN WEHR. Der Neubau, 22. Einheit einer überaus erfolgreichen Sietas-Serie, war einfach und effektiv, *ein 'Schiff, das lesen und schreiben*

First ship from the Sietas yard

In the summer of 1955 one of Oskar Wehr's dreams came true. He ordered a new ship to be built by Johann Jacob Sietas in Neuenfelde. Within the space of two weeks Wehr had managed to get the necessary guarantee from the regional Hamburg government. This was a matter to be proud of, as he needed his ship as quickly as possible. Sietas congratulated Wehr on arranging for financial back-up so quickly, but added that other owners had also done the same. Sietas assured Wehr that delivery time would be 18 months. Peter Döhle, who was still working for Robert Bornhofen KG at the time, knew of several owners who had ordered the same ship's type (a 424-GRT single-decker) and was interested in similar ships being built to fulfill his contract. Döhle promised to exert his influence where he could to obtain an earlier delivery, whilst Bauer & Hauschildt KG, Wehr's brokers, predicted he would 'never' get the ship. On the recommendation of a man from MaK, Wehr decided to change brokers and go over to Döhle at Bornhofen, largely because they had promised him gross freight earnings of DM 450,000 a year and quick delivery of a new ship. The latter took longer than Döhle had promised. On 14th November 1957 Oskar Wehr took delivery of the JÜRGEN WEHR, the coaster named after his son. The new ship was No. 22 in a series of very successful ships produced by Sietas. She was simple and efficient, in fact a ship which could 'read and write' and which produced good earnings.

JÜRGEN WEHR (1), nun verlängert und mit einem Pfostenpaar vor der Brücke, beim Holzladen in Finnland.

mv JÜRGEN WEHR (1) after jumboising, with Samson posts in front of superstructure, loading timber in Finland.

konnte' und gutes Geld verdiente. Dennoch fuhr Oskar Wehr weiter zur See. Größtenteils auf dem Neubau, er löste aber auch seinen Kapitän Pries auf der HELGA WEHR ab. Üblicherweise in Brunsbüttel tauschten der Reeder und sein Kapitän die Fahrzeuge. Oskar Wehr übernahm das Schiff, Kapitän Pries bekam für die Dauer seines Urlaubs das Auto seines Reeders. Bei einer solchen Reise fand Oskar Wehr seine HELGA WEHR fast überladen vor, man konnte kaum über das Holz hinwegschauen. Weil es aufbriste, gab Kapitän Wehr die Anweisung, alle Spannschrauben, die die Holzlaschings nicht mehr stramm zogen, nachzuziehen und steif zu legen. Auf seine Bemerkung, „ihr habt ja gut geladen" mußte er sich vom Steuermann anhören, „kaum ist der Reeder an Bord, macht er sich die Büxen voll". Nach der anstrengenden Autofahrt nach Brunsbüttel

In spite of this Oskar Wehr continued to go to sea, mostly on his new ship, but occasionally he also relieved the Master of the HELGA WEHR, Captain Pries. It was the practice for owner and master to swap over vessels at Brunsbüttel. Oskar Wehr took command of the ship and Captain Pries had the use of the owner's car for his shore leave. On one such trip Oskar Wehr found the HELGA WEHR nearly overloaded, the view ahead virtually obstructed. When a wind blew up Captain Wehr ordered all the turnbuckles on the cargo lashings on deck to be tightened and secured. When he remarked *"you're well loaded"* the Mate replied: *"As soon as the owner's on board he wets his pants."* Wehr turned in to rest after a tiring journey to Brunsbüttel (there were no good main roads then as there are now). Back on deck he found the lashings

(damals gab es keine ausgebauten Bundesstraßen) legte er sich hin, und fand, als er wieder an Deck war, immer noch lose Lashings vor. Der Steuermann weigerte sich, bei der rauhen See an Deck zu arbeiten, und erst auf massives Wiederholen der Kapitänsanweisung machte sich der Steuermann mit zwei Mann, gut angeseilt, an die Arbeit. Dennoch brachen vor Terschelling auf einer Seite die Deckslaststützen, die Ladung verrutschte, und mit 45 Grad Schlagseite blieb das Schiff liegen. Über das Farbenspind und die Toilette lief jedoch Wasser in den Maschinenraum, die Lenzpumpen kamen aber gegen die Wassermassen an.

Zwar wollte der Steuermann die anderen Lashings lösen und die Deckslast über Bord kippen, das aber ließ der Reeder nicht zu. Das Schiff lag sicher genug und konnte auch mit Schlagseite seinen Bestimmungshafen Great Yarmouth erreichen. Das vor Yarmouth liegende Feuerschiff OUTER GABBARD schoß angesichts der stark überliegenden HELGA WEHR zwar Notsignale, was man an Bord des Hamburger Schiffes nicht verstand. Es war nicht zu erkennen, daß das Feuerschiff in Not war. Great Yarmouth Reede lag voll von Windliegern, der Lotse weigerte sich, das Schiff mit seinen 45 Grad Schlagseite in den Hafen zu lotsen.

„Ich sagte zum Lotsen: 'ich brauche Sie nicht, nennen Sie mir einen Platz und ich fahr allein hin'. Nachdem wir das Schiff durch Lenzen des Backbordtanks – was man in solcher Situation eigentlich nicht macht, aber was sollte auf Reede noch passieren – etwas höher und etwas gerade getrimmt hatten, und den Lotsen eindringlich bearbeitet hatten, durften wir einlaufen."

Drei Tage später erreichte JÜRGEN WEHR Great Yarmouth, und die Lotsen berichteten

were still loose. The Mate refused to work on deck in such rough seas and only after repeated orders was persuaded to carry out the work with two other men – all with safety ropes. Off Terschelling the stanchions securing the cargo on deck broke on one side, the cargo shifted and the ship had to continue with a 45° list. Water still continued to enter the engine room via the paint store and the lavatory, but the bilge pumps managed to keep the water at bay.

The Mate was all for cutting the remaining lashing ropes and jettisoning the deck cargo but the owner refused. The ship was still safe enough and managed to reach its destination, Great Yarmouth. When it sighted the HELGA WEHR, the lightship OUTER GABBARD off Great Yarmouth sent off distress signals, which were misunderstood by the HELGA WEHR. To all intents and purposes the lightship was not in distress. The roads off Great Yarmouth were full of ships seeking shelter. The pilot refused to take a ship with a list of 45° into port. *"So I told the pilot I don't need him, I'll get to the berth myself if he told me where it was. So we righted the ship and trimmed her as best we could by pumping off the port tanks – not something one should strictly do in a situation like that – but not much could have happened to us anyway in the roads. After using our powers of persuasion on the pilot, we were given permission to enter the port."*

Three days later the JÜRGEN WEHR sailed into Great Yarmouth and the pilots told the master, Karl Schwarz, about the "crazy captain" on his sister ship, the HELGA WEHR. "That's my owner," Schwarz told the speechless pilots. Three days after that Oskar Wehr

Mit dieser Schlagseite lief die HELGA WEHR in Great Yarmouth ein.

mv HELGA WEHR entering Great Yarmouth with a heavy list.

dem Kapitän Karl Schwarz vom 'crazy captain' of your sistervessel HELGA WEHR',
„That's my owner"
antwortete er den sprachlosen Lotsen. Drei Tage später war Oskar Wehr Gast in einem ganz feudalen Klub der Stadt, Lotsen und Hafenkapitän entschuldigten sich. Wehrs wahren Beweggrund für die Schlagseite erfuhren sie nicht. Der lag noch nicht lange zurück. Unter Kapitän Wilhelm Grönke war die HELGA WEHR mit voller Deckslast Holz in Richtung Westen gefahren. In der Elbmündung hatte das Schiff Südwest 9-10 Beaufort, der vor der Emsmündung auf Nordwest elf-zwölf aufbriste. Grönke lief in die Emsmündung ein, ein Manöver, das zum Verlust der Deckslast führte. Die Versicherung zitierte den Reeder ins Büro, beklagte ihren Verlust. Der konnte nur sagen, ihm wäre das nicht passiert. Mit einem kurzen, „ja, ja die

was invited to one of the best clubs in town, where the port captain and pilots apologized. They never knew the real reason for the list in Wehr's ship. Shortly before, the HELGA WEHR, under Captain Wilhelm Grönke, had been heading west with a full cargo of timber on deck. On reaching the mouth of the Elbe a southwesterly wind blew up at force 9 to 10, increasing to northwest force 11 to 12 off the Ems estuary. Grönke sailed into the Ems estuary and the manoeuvre sent his deck cargo overboard. The insurance company summoned the owner to their offices, demanding an explanation for the loss. All Wehr could say was that it would not have happened to him. He was dismissed with the curt reply: *"Yes of course, the best seamen are always on shore."* After such a short space of time he could not afford to lose another

besten Seeleute sind immer an Land" wurde er entlassen. So kurze Zeit später *konnte* er es sich gar nicht leisten, die Deckslast zu verlieren. So kam die Geschichte vom Helden von Great Yarmouth zustande – die schiefliegende HELGA WEHR sorgte nämlich für Schlagzeilen.

1960 vergrößerte sich die Flotte, ohne daß ein Schiff dazukam. JÜRGEN WEHR wurde verlängert und konnte nun bei 498 BRT 834 Tonnen tragen. 1963 kaufte Oskar Wehr von der Hamburger Poseidon Schiffahrt GmbH deren Singledecker HOHENBUCHEN. Das Schiff reihte er als MARIANNE WEHR in die Flotte ein, die nun aus drei Einheiten bestand. In der Größe und der Verwendbarkeit paßte das Schiff zur JÜRGEN WEHR, gehörte aber, da von Peters in Wewelsfleth gebaut, zu einem anderen Typ.

deckload of cargo. That is how the story of the Hero of Great Yarmouth arose. The list on the HELGA WEHR hit the headlines.

The fleet was expanded in 1960, not by the purchase of another vessel but by having the JÜRGEN WEHR extended to carry 498 GRT and 834 tonnes. Then in 1963 Oskar Wehr bought the single-decker HOHENBUCHEN from the Hamburg shipping company Poseidon Schiffahrt GmbH. She was renamed the MARIANNE WEHR and was the third ship in the Wehr fleet. Her size and use were the same as the JÜRGEN WEHR but she was of a different type, having been built at the Peters yard in Wewelsfleth.

Durch Einfügen einer 7,7 m langen Mittschiffssektion wurde JÜRGEN WEHR (1) von der Bauwerft verlängert.

mv JÜRGEN WEHR (1) at the builders' yard, being lengthened by inserting a 7.7m midship section.

Jürgen, Marianne, Helga und Oskar Wehr auf HELGA WEHR (1), oben links. HELGA WEHR (1) und JÜRGEN WEHR (1) am Kai der Sietas-Werft, unten links. Familie Wehr: (vlnr) Oskar und Helga Wehr, Tante Luischen, Cousine Luise Wehr, eine Besucherin und Wilhelm Wehr, vorne Jürgen und Marianne Wehr (oben rechts) und zwei Ansichten von der MARIANNE WEHR (darunter).

Upper left: Jürgen, Marianne, Helga und Oskar Wehr on board mv HELGA WEHR (1). Lower left: mvs HELGA WEHR (1) and JÜRGEN WEHR (1) double-banked at the Sietas shipyard. Upper right: The Wehr familiy: from right to left Oskar and Helga Wehr, aunt Luischen, cousin Luise Wehr, a visitor and Wilhelm Wehr; front row: Jürgen and Marianne Wehr. Centre and lower right: two views of mv MARIANNE WEHR.

Die MARIANNE WEHR fuhr leider nur kurze Zeit unter der blau-gelben Wehr-Flagge. Am 14. Oktober 1963 befand sich das Schiff unter Kapitän Pries auf der Reise von Flixborough nach Lübeck mit Splitt, als es in der Elbmündung in einen Orkan geriet. In den frühen Morgenstunden meldete sich Kapitän Pries in seiner Not bei seinem Reeder, der verzweifelt versuchte, sofort schnelle Rettungsmaßnahmen einzuleiten. Auch mit seinem langjährigen Besatzungsmitglied Andreas Petersen – er war, solange es die Maschinenleistungen zuließen, als zweiter Maschinist auf Fischdampfern gefahren und zu Oskar Wehr zurückgekehrt – sprach der Reeder noch: „Oskar, verlaß Dich auf mich, wi mokt das schon". Kurz danach überlief eine schwere See den Frachter von achtern und brachte ihn zum Kentern. Als dann gegen sieben Uhr die Rettungshubschrauber den vermuteten Unfallort erreichten, war es zu spät. MARIANNE WEHR war mit ihrer neunköpfigen Besatzung untergegangen:

Kapitän Heinz Pries
Steuermann Jürgen Haider
Maschinist Andreas Petersen
Matrose Egon Langhein
Leichtmatrose Jürgen Boderius
Jungmann Harald Hansen
Jungmann Reinhard Scholz
Jungmann Peter Berger und
Kochsmaat Günter Schwarz

hatten ein Seemannsgrab gefunden. –
Der Verlust traf die Familie Wehr und insbesondere den Kapitän und Reeder schwer. Als kleine Küstenschiffsreederei hatte man zu seinen Besatzungen fast familiäre Beziehungen. Noch Jahrzehnte später war ihm bei den Schilderungen des Unterganges anzumerken, wie sehr ihn dieses Unglück getroffen hatte.

Unfortunately she only sailed for a short time under the blue-and-yellow company flag. The ship was on a trip from Flixborough to Lübeck, under Captain Pries, with a cargo of stone chippings when, on 14th October 1963, she ran into a hurricane-force gale in the mouth of the river Elbe. Captain Pries called up the owner in the early hours of the morning. Wehr tried to organise rescue operations as quickly as he could and even spoke to Andreas Petersen, a crew member of long standing who had served as Second Engineer on fishing trawlers as long as his licence had permitted, but had since returned to Wehr. Petersen told Wehr: "Oskar, you can rely on me. We'll make it." Shortly after that a heavy sea from aft washed over the vessel, causing her to capsize. By the time rescue helicopters arrived at the presumed location of the accident (at around 7 a.m.), it was too late. The MARIANNE WEHR and her crew of nine had sunk. The crew who had gone down were:

Captain: Heinz Pries
Mate: Jürgen Haider
Engineer: Andreas Petersen
Seaman: Egon Langhein
Ordinary Seaman: Jürgen Boderius
Apprentice: Harald Hansen
Apprentice: Reinhard Scholz
Apprentice: Peter Berger
Sub-Cook: Günter Schwarz

It was a great loss to the Wehr family and, above all, Captain and Owner Oskar Wehr, as crews are almost part of the family in small coastal shipping companies. Many years after the event Wehr could still not hide his emotions when the incident was mentioned.

Mehr Urlaub für die Seeleute – mehr Schiffe

Zwischen 1965 und 1970 änderten sich die Arbeitszeitbedingungen und die Tarifverträge. Kapitäne, Offiziere und Besatzungen bekamen nun wesentlich mehr Urlaub, so daß es dem Reeder nicht mehr möglich war, allein Vertretungen für seine Kapitäne zu fahren. Für drei Schiffe mußte man etwa vier Besatzungen haben. Für die untergegangene MARIANNE WEHR orderte die Reederei bei Sietas einen 499-BRT-Freidecker, der am Silvestertag des Jahres 1964 auf Probefahrt ging. Er wurde auf den Namen der 1959 geborenen zweiten Tochter GABRIELE WEHR getauft. Noch vor Ablieferung dieses modernen Schiffes erhielt Johann Jacob Sietas den Auftrag zum Bau einer neuen HELGA WEHR. Dieser Neubau kam als Wechselschiff mit 499 BRT bzw. 1190 BRT in Fahrt und wurde das neue Flaggschiff. Mit diesem modernen Stückgutfrachter konnte Wehr seine Definition, Küstenschiffahrt findet überall statt, durchsetzen. Da die Schiffe Eisklasse E 3 erhielten, entsprachen sie automatisch den Anforderungen für Große Fahrt, auch wenn ihr Fahrterlaubnisschein aus Besetzungsgründen nur für die Kleine oder Mittlere Fahrt ausgestellt war. Das machte sie aber auch für die Winterfahrt nach Skandinavien interessant, ein Ausrüstungsmerkmal, das viel Geld brachte. Die erste HELGA WEHR gehörte noch immer zur Flotte und stand seit 1962 unter dem Kommando von Friedrich Heidemann, einem Rheinländer aus Mönchengladbach. Mit ihm war Oskar Wehr seit dem A 5-Lehrgang in Hamburg gut befreundet, und der Lebensweg der beiden lief trotz unterschiedlicher Entwicklung mehrfach zusam-

More shore leave – more ships

Between 1965 and 1970 changes occurred in working hours and tariff agreements. Masters, officers and ordinary crew members were given substantially longer periods of leave, so Wehr was no longer able to stand in for them alone. Three ships required about four crews. To replace the MARIANNE WEHR the company ordered a 499-GRT open shelter-decker at the Sietas yard, which went on her trial run on New Year's Eve 1964. She was named the GABRIELE WEHR, after the owner's second daughter who was born in 1959. Even before delivery had been taken of this modern ship Wehr placed the order for a new ship, HELGA WEHR, with Johann Jacob Sietas. She was commissioned as an open/closed shelter-decker of 499/1190 GRT. She was to be the company's new flag ship. With her, Wehr actually practised his motto 'coastal shipping can be carried out anywhere.' Ships of her type were classified under Ice Class 3, so she automatically qualified to run as an ocean-going vessel, in spite of the fact that her sailing permits were frequently restricted to coastal or medium-range trading, due to crew numbers. Her classification made winter trading to and from Scandinavia an interesting prospect and was an investment which later paid off.

As from 1962 the first HELGA WEHR, still part of the fleet, had been under the command of Friedrich Heidemann. He had been born in Mönchengladbach in the Rhineland region. He had been a good friend of Oskar Wehr ever since they had sat for their coastal skip-

Das jüngste der drei Wehr-Kinder, Gabriele Wehr, taufte den zweiten Neubau auf ihren Namen, Johann Jacob Sietas half ihr dabei.

Gabriele Wehr, youngest of three children, naming the second newbuilding after her own name, with Johann Jacob Sietas assisting.

men. Heidemann fuhr nach dem Kriege bei der Reederei Reckmann, deren kleine Seeschiffe er mit seinem Patent als I. Offizier fahren konnte, war dann bei der Polizei und heuerte später bei Döhle an. Dort hatte er Schwierigkeiten mit seinem Glauben. Er glaubte, eine große Menge Zigaretten nicht verzollen zu müssen und mußte eine Menge Zoll nachbezahlen. Er erinnerte sich an die Freundschaft zu Wehr. Er fuhr zunächst zusammen mit einem ganz jungen Kapitän als Steuermann auf der HELGA WEHR und übernahm das Schiff dann als Kapitän. Als Perspektive war ihm die spätere Übernahme des Schiffes zum attraktiven Kaufpreis von 27.000 Mark zugesagt worden. Voraussetzung war, daß der Frachter zuvor netto 420.000 Mark auffahren müßte. Kapitän Heidemann erhielt darüber hin-

pers' licenses together in Hamburg. Their paths kept crossing at different points in their lives. After the War Heidemann became a captain with the Reckmann shipping company, where he was able to sail as Chief Officer with his coastal skipper's license. Good faith ran him into trouble. He had to pay a large amount of Customs' duty for a large quantity of cigarettes. Remembering Wehr, he started as Chief Mate under a very young Master on the HELGA WEHR and later took over as Master. Wehr had promised to sell him the ship at an attractive price (DM 27,000) but not until the ship had made net freight earnings of altogether DM 420,000. Over and above this Captain Heidemann received normal wages and leave, according to the tariffs

Man to, man to
de Tied is knapp
uns Schipp mutt unbedingt hüt ar
wi heft al teuft de ganze Tied
un endlich is dat nu so wiet.
Wi wärn uns ja im kloren,
dat wi en beten to leüben harn
aber düsse ganze Tied
dat geiht uns doch to wiet.
Wenn wi to rechten Tied
dat Schipp nich kriegt
geiht uns dat bannig schlecht,
da wi en Finanzamt heft.

Wenn wi dat Schipp uns so betracht
dan seht wi wat de Warft vollbracht
in 10 Doog bud se da Schipp
as en wores Meisterstück
De Boos und sien Lüd
sind bekannt för gode Arbeit hüt
de but dat Schipp so torecht,
dat wi dat mit allen Schikanen heft
un gift uns so de Gewähr
uns Schipp kommt al Tied
in sien Heimat wedder her
und wi seht dat so
as Gorch Fock dat säh
„Seefahrt ist not "

Nu wünscht wi „GABRIELE WEHR"
alltied gode Fahrt.

Links: Der Taufspruch für GABRIELE WEHR (1).
Rechts: Helga, Oskar, Marianne, Gabriele und Jürgen Wehr sowie Johann Jacob Sietas bei der Tauffeier.
GABRIELE WEHR (1) im Englischen Kanal.

Left: The naming poem for my GABRIELE WEHR (1).
Upper right: Helga, Oskar, Marianne, Gabriele and Jürgen Wehr and Johann Jacob Sietas celebrating the naming of mv GABRIELE WEHR (1), pictured below in the Channel

aus tarifliche Heuer und Urlaub. Sein Freund Oskar sicherte ihm Offenlegung der Bilanzen zu. Als dieses Schiff im Februar 1966 den Namen für das neue Flaggschiff hergeben mußte, erfolgte eine Umbenennung in ILSE H. 1968 ging der Frachter in das Eigentum Heidemanns über. Danach fuhr er allerdings nur noch ein gutes Jahr. Am 2. April 1969 ging ILSE H nach einem Wassereinbruch vor Hoek van Holland verloren. Beim Bergungsversuch offenbarte sich das Alter, sie brach auseinander. Die Form und die Verbände des ehemaligen Fischdampfers

at the time. As proof his friend Oskar promised him free access to his books. When, in February 1966, the ship had to pass her name on to the new flag ship, she was renamed the ILSE H. In 1968 she became the property of Heidemann but only remained in active service for about another year. On 2nd April 1969 the ship was lost off the Hook of Holland, having sprung a leak. Her age was against her during the rescue operations, as she fell apart. The line and joints of the former trawler were still strong but the plating was not. The

Das Wechselschiff HELGA WEHR (2).   *The open/closed shelterdecker HELGA WEHR (2)*

waren zwar sehr stark, aber die Platten nicht mehr. Das Schiff mußte als Totalverlust abgeschrieben werden.

Die neue HELGA WEHR (2) führte Kapitän Wehr nur noch eine Reise, die Tätigkeit als Reeder nahm ihn nun voll in Anspruch. Rund zwanzig Jahre ist er als Kapitän oder Schiffer gefahren. Zu seinen Kommandos gehörten eine Siebelfähre (ohne Patent) und das vierzehntägige Befehligen eines Schleppers im Hafen von Aarhus. Mit 24 Jahren stand er dann am Ruder seines ersten eigenen Schiffes. Nach der ständigen Fahrtzeit schlossen sich häufige Urlaubsvertretungen an. Urlaube verbrachte die Familie Wehr bis dahin grundsätzlich an Bord.

ship was written off as a total loss.

The new HELGA WEHR (2) was under Captain Wehr's command for only one voyage. Demands were increasing on him as a shipowner. He had sailed as a master or skipper for about twenty years. The vessels he had commanded included a Siebel ferry (without a licence) and he had been in charge of a harbour tug in Aarhus for a fortnight. At the age of 24 he had taken over the wheel of his first own ship. After being at sea for years he started doing relief trips for masters on leave. This meant that until then the Wehr family had always spent its holidays on board ships.

Der Kapitänsreeder und seine Kapitäne

Gutes Personal war und ist für jeden Reedereibetrieb wichtig. Oskar Wehr:
„Beim Aufbau meines Schiffahrtsbetriebes war ich natürlich auf die Mitarbeit meiner Bordbesatzungen angewiesen. Nach dem erwähnten Kapitän Schwarz übernahm Johannes Cassau die Schiffsführung von JÜRGEN WEHR. Cassau war Jahrgang 1921 und nur auf Küstenschiffen gefahren, davon zehn Jahre als Kapitän. Er brachte das richtige Verständnis mit und trug alle Erneuerungen an Bord und die Erweiterungen des Fahrtgebietes mit. Er besuchte dafür noch einmal die Seefahrtsschule und erweiterte sein Patent. Anfangs fuhren wir in Nord- und Ostsee, dann auch durch die Biskaya, an die französische Küste, im gesamten Mittelmeer und an Nordafrikas Küsten. Mit der Fertigstellung der HELGA WEHR (2) konnte ich durchsetzen, daß unsere Gilden auch andere Fahrtgebiete und Schiffsgrößen aufnahmen. Nach und nach stießen wir in andere Fahrtgebiete, meine Kapitäne erweiterten alle auf der Seefahrtsschule ihr Patent für große Schiffe und weltweite Fahrt. Meine Mitarbeiter tragen erheblich Anteil am Ausbau der Flotte, vor allem die aus der Küstenschiffahrt stammenden Kapitäne. 1962 kam Gerhard Werner zu uns. Zunächst als Steuermann, aber bereits mit 24 Jahren wurde er aufgrund seiner Tüchtigkeit Kapitän. Er steht auch jetzt noch in den Diensten seiner Reederei. Seine Kollegen nennen ihn den 'Starkapitän'. Die gut 20 Jahre alte JANNE WEHR sieht noch heute wie ein Neubau aus, so pflegt Kapitän Werner sein Schiff. Wie alle guten Seeleute kommt er aus dem

Owner-Master and his Captains

Good staff are always vital for any shipping company.
Oskar Wehr: "When I started building up the company I was dependent on the co-operation of my crews on board. Successor to Captain Schwarz as master of the JÜRGEN WEHR was Johannes Cassau. Cassau was born in 1921 and had only sailed on coastal ships, ten years as a master. He had the right kind of understanding and supported all the necessary changes which were made on board. This included expanding the company's trading areas. He went back to college and took a higher licence. We started by trading in the North Sea and the Baltic, then gradually moved to the Bay of Biscay, French coasts and the entire Mediterranean and North African coasts. Once the HELGA WEHR (2) was in commission I persuaded the guilds

Bis zum 'Paketzeitalter' wurde Holz Brett für Brett gestaut.
Until the age of packages, timber was manually stowed board by board.

Die Brücke von GABRIELE WEHR (2).
The bridge of mv GABRIELE WEHR (2).

Binnenland, hat aber noch die alte Schule der Küstenschiffahrt mitgemacht.

1965 begann Kapitän Franz Hintz, Sohn eines Küstenschiffers, seine Fahrtzeit bei uns. Empfohlen wurde er von seinem väterlichen Freund, Kapitän Bröcker. Franz Hintz kam von der Horn-Linie, wo er als Erster Offizier fuhr. Nach kurzer Fahrtzeit als Steuermann übernahm er die neue HELGA WEHR. Da er A 6 hat, brachte er viele neue Erfahrungen mit. Wenn es sein mußte, konnte er seinen Meistern oder Ingenieuren die 'richtigen' Anweisungen geben, er war ein durchaus tüchtiger Mann, der sich Ende 1993 in den Ruhestand setzte.

Kapitän Hans-Dieter Främbs mit dem Patent AM begann 1975 bei uns, auch er ist ein tüchtiger Mitarbeiter und machte mit unserem Spezialschiff SIGRID WEHR sogar eine Reise um die Welt. Jetzt ist er Kapitän des Ro/Ro-Frachters GABRIELE WEHR. Eine Reparatur an der Maschine von HELGA WEHR inmitten der Wirren des Bürgerkrieges in Beirut 1975 leitete er. Ich war einige Tage dort und erkannte seine

to extend our insurance cover to include other trading areas and larger vessels. All our masters went back to nautical college and took higher licences so that they could command bigger ships and sail worldwide. Our staff made a vital contribution towards expanding the fleet, particularly the masters who had grown up on coasters.

In 1962 Gerhard Werner joined us. He began as Chief Mate but was so competent, he was promoted to Master at the age of 24. He is still with the company. His colleagues call him 'the star Captain'. Captain Werner takes such good care of his ship, the JANNE WEHR, that she looks as good as new after almost 20 years. Like all good seamen he was born inland but underwent standard training on coastal ships.

In 1965 we were joined by Captain Franz Hintz, the son of a coastal skipper. He was recommended by his father's friend, Captain Bröcker. Franz Hintz came from the Horn Line, where he had been Chief Officer. After only a short time as Mate he took over command of the new HELGA WEHR. His Master's license qualified him to command ocean-going ships, so he brought a lot of additional experience with him when he came. He was a very competent master, who knew when and how to instruct his boatswains and engineers. He retired at the end of 1993.

In 1975 we engaged Captain Hans-Dieter Främbs, who had a coastal Captain's license. He is another competent member of our staff, who has sailed around the world with the SIGRID WEHR, our roll on-roll off ship. At the time of writing he is in command of another roll on-roll off vessel, the GABRIELE WEHR. In 1975, in the middle of the civil war in Beirut,

JÜRGEN WEHR (1) nach der Verlängerung (oben). Besatzungsfoto von GABRIELE WEHR (1) mit Kapitän Johannes Cassau (links neben dem Koch), ganz links Gerhard Werner

mv JÜRGEN WEHR (1) after jumboising (above); The crew of mv GABRIELE WEHR (1) with Captain Johannes Cassau (to the left of the cook); Gerhard Werner on the far left.

Schwierigkeiten und Gefahren. Es gab keine Werft, keine Werkstatt, und dann wurde noch scharf geschossen. Morgens lagen Granatsplitter an Deck. Die neue Kurbelwelle wurde mit Hilfe von eingeflogenen Monteuren unter der Leitung des Kapitäns eingebaut.

Unsere Kapitäne sind die 'Macher' an Bord, und wie in früheren Zeiten leitet der Kapitän das Schiff. Gewiß haben wir auch im Maschinenbereich tüchtige Mitarbeiter, denn ohne sie würden die Maschinen nicht laufen, aber die Seele des Schiffes ist und bleibt der Kapitän. Wenn er dann noch aus der Küstenschiffahrt kommt, ist er universell ausgebildet.

Auch das Vertrauen meiner Partner und Partenreeder Helga und Hans Werner Schultz sowie Arnold Fölsch erleichterten mir meinen Aufbau und meine Arbeit, denn es bildete sich schnell ein gemeinsames Interesse.

Ich hatte das Glück, daß meine Kapitäne voll hinter der Reederei standen und wir es als gemeinsames Ziel ansahen, die deutsche Schiffahrt leistungsfähig zu gestalten. Erfreulicherweise habe ich mit allen Kapitänen noch Verbindung, auch mit Kapitän Schröder, der derzeit die Seefahrtschule von Tuvalu im Pazifik leitet. Junge Leute, die bei mir fuhren, setzen sich noch heute mit mir in Verbindung, selbst wenn sie zwischenzeitlich Hafenkapitän in einem Hafen der USA geworden sind.

Captain Främbs supervised a major engine repair job on the HELGA WEHR. I was there for a few days, and so realised the difficulties and dangers he had to encounter. There was no repair yard, no workshop and they were in the line of fire. Shrapnel would litter the deck every morning. The master supervised the fitting of the new crankshaft by engineers who had been flown in for the job.

Our captains are all men of action on board. They still manage our ships in the traditional sense. Of course we have very able men in the technical department too. Without good engineers the engines would not run at all. But the Master still is, and always will be, the soul of the ship. If on top of that he has a background of coastal shipping, then he has had a thorough, all-round training.

My work and the growth of the company owe a great deal to the mutual trust I have with my partners and co-owners, Helga and Hans-Werner Schultz and Arnold Fölsch, and to the support they have given me in building up the company and my work. Jointly we have developed identical interests. I was fortunate enough to have masters who backed the company to the full and shared my conviction that we had to make our own contribution towards making German shipping efficient. It is gratifying to keep in touch with all the masters who have been with us, including Captain Schröder, who is currently head of the nautical college in Tuvalu in the South Pacific. Young men who used to sail on our ships still contact me, even if they are now harbour masters in the United States."

Ein Schottland-Auftrag scheiterte an einem Ultimatum

Mitte der sechziger Jahre gab es für deutsche Reedereien die Möglichkeit, aus dem sogenannten Devisenabkommen mit Großbritannien günstige Kredite zu bekommen. Diese von der Bundesregierung bereitgestellten Mittel sollten die Zahlungsbilanz mit Großbritannien, die durch die Stationierung der Rheinarmee in Deutschland nicht ausgeglichen war, mehr in die Waage bringen. Die in Dortmund ansässige Retzlaff Reederei hatte bei der Clelands Shipbuilding Ltd. in Wallsend an der Tyne einen 1598 BRT großen Singledecker mit Geschirr bestellt, der 3100 Tonnen tragen sollte. Schiffsmakler Hans Schirren hatte Wehr für diesen Typ interessiert, und man war in feste Auftragsverhandlungen eingestiegen. Werft, Reederei und Makler trafen sich meist am Londoner Flughafen, der lag etwa auf halbem Wege zwischen Hamburg und Wallsend. Wehr hatte schon verschiedene Verbesserungen und Aufrüstungen durchgesetzt – trotz des schon vereinbarten Festpreises. Unmittelbar vor Vertragsunterzeichnung verlor der Werftdirektor jedoch die Nerven, wollte eine letzte Änderung nicht mehr hinnehmen und gab Wehr nur noch die Möglichkeit zu einem 'Take it or leave it' des letzten Angebotes. Schirren sagte zu seinem Prinzipal: „Herr Wehr, lassen Sie sich das nicht gefallen" – obwohl er sich damit um ein gutes Geschäft brachte. Oskar Wehr ließ es und er brauchte den Entschluß nicht zu bereuen, wie die Erfahrungen der Retzlaff-Reederei mit ihrem England-Neubau später bewiesen.

An ultimatum

In the mid-'sixties the so-called currency agreement between Great Britain and West Germany gave German owners the chance to make use of attractive credit terms. The funds available from the Federal government were not adequately compensated for by the British Army of the Rhine, which was stationed in Germany. This was an attempt to balance out payments. The Retzlaff shipping company, which was based in Dortmund, had ordered a 1598-GRT single-decker, equipped with its own cargo-handling gear and capable of carrying 3,100 tdw, from Clelands Shipbuilding Ltd. of Wallsend-on-Tyne. Hans Schirren, the shipbroker, had aroused Wehr's interest in this type of ship and contract negotiations followed. Shipbuilders' representatives, owners and brokers would usually meet at Heathrow Airport, approximately half way between Hamburg and Wallsend. In spite of the price already being fixed, Wehr had succeeded in inserting a number of improvements into the contract. However, just before the contract was to be signed the shipyard manager lost his nerve and refused to accept the final amendment. Wehr's only option was to 'take it or leave it'. Schirren told his client *"Mr Wehr, you can't put up with that,"* although he himself was about to lose good business. Oskar Wehr left it and never regretted the decision.

Wehr still continued to expand his fleet. A sales broker offered the 1471-GRT single-decker FALLSUND. She had been completed as the FLEETWING in 1956, at the Meyer-Werft in Papenburg. The Finnish owners eventually agreed to a reduced down price of DM

Die Flottenausbaupläne wurden dennoch weiter verfolgt. Ein Verkaufsmakler bot den 1471 BRT-Singledecker FALLSUND an, ein Schiff, das die Meyer-Werft in Papenburg 1956 als FLEETWING abgeliefert hatte. Die finnischen Eigner ließen sich auf 700.000 DM herunterhandeln, die geplante Verlängerung des Schiffes und die Umrüstung bei der Meyer-Werft auf deutsche Vorschriften kamen auf 500.000 DM. Der Einbau eines kleinen Zwischendecks, um auf günstige Vermessungswerte zu kommen, war darin eingeschlossen. Das Schiff kam dann 1968 als HUGO SELMER, so benannt nach dem Vater von Frau Wehr, in Fahrt. Kapitän Grube fuhr mit dem Frachter vorwiegend Kohle nach französischen Häfen, gelegentlich andere Bulkladungen wie Schwefel, Pottasche, Kies usw. Besonders die Schwefelladungen haben dem Schiff sehr zugesetzt, wie der Vergleich der Schallergebnisse bei Übergabe und vor dem Verkauf offenlegten.

700,000. Extension work on the ship and other adaptations, so that she would conform to German regulations, cost another DM 500,000. This included construction of a small tweendeck which resulted in better measurements. She was taken into commission in 1968 and named the HUGO SELMER after Mrs. Wehr's father. Under Captain Grube she mainly carried coal to French ports but also transported other bulk cargoes such as sulphur, potash, gravel, etc.. The cargoes of sulphur affected the ship particularly badly, as comparative sonar tests later showed prior to her delivery and sale.

HUGO SELMER wartet mit einer Holzladung auf Einlauforder.

mv HUGO SELMER, with a full cargo of timber, awaiting orders to enter port.

Umzug vom Sofa in ein eigenes Büro

1967 wurde aus der Personenfirma Oskar Wehr die Firma Oskar Wehr Kommanditgesellschaft. Das Büro zog vom Wohnhaus in Rissen, wo die Familie 1962 einen geräumigen Neubau bezogen hatte, in ein Bürohaus in der Neuen Großen Bergstraße in Altona. Aus der 'Sofareederei' war ein voll funktionsfähiger Schifffahrtsbetrieb mit Inspektion, Buchhaltung und Personalabteilung entstanden. Nur die Befrachtung machte man nicht selbst. Wehr hatte sie Adolf Feindt, einem ehemaligen Mitarbeiter der Firma Döhle übertragen, der sich mit dem Transmar Schiffahrtskontor selbständig gemacht hatte. Feindt, so Oskar Wehr, war weit und breit der beste Makler, ein hervorragender Verhandlungspartner, der außergewöhnliche Ergebnisse erzielte. Den einzigen kleinen Schwachpunkt Feindts- den hat ja jeder – wußte man im gegenseitigen Einvernehmen zu umschiffen. 1969 kam der Reedersohn Jürgen in die väterliche Firma. Nach seinem Schulabschluß hatte er die Handelsschule besucht, bei der Hamburger Reederei Hans Krüger den Beruf des Reedereikaufmannes gelernt und schließlich ein Jahr im walisischen Cardiff die Englischkenntnisse erweitert und Erfahrungen gesammelt.

Mitte der sechziger Jahre hatte ein umfassender Strukturwandel nicht nur die Seeschiffahrt, sondern auch die Küstenschiffahrt erfaßt. 1966 kam das erste deutsche Containerschiff, ein Kümo, in Fahrt, und in Skandinavien stellte man die Holzverladungen auf standardisierte Pakete um. Sowohl Container wie auch die Holzpakete erforderten einen völlig neuen Schiffstyp: Frachter mit großen Lukenöffnungen und möglichst

The move to a proper office

In 1967 the Oskar Wehr company changed its status from a one-man business to a Kommanditgesellschaft, a limited partnership. The offices moved from the spacious house the Wehrs had built in Rissen in 1962, to a proper office building in the Neue Grosse Bergstrasse in Altona. The company became a fully-fledged shipping company, with separate management, accounting and personnel departments. Only the chartering was still left to others. Wehr had entrusted this sector to Adolf Feindt, who had formerly worked for the Döhle company, but then started up his own business, the Transmar Schiffahrtskontor. In Oskar Wehr's opinion Feindt was the best shipbroker far and wide and an excellent negotiator, who achieved extraordinarily good results. By mutual consent Feindt's only weak point – and everybody has one – was ignored. Jürgen Wehr joined his father's company in 1969. After finishing school he had attended commercial college, then did a commercial apprenticeship with the Hamburg shipowner Hans Krüger. Following that he spent a year in Cardiff to improve his English and gain experience.

By the 'sixties comprehensive structural changes were affecting ocean-going and short-sea shipping alike. The first German container vessel – a coastal vessel – was taken into commission in 1966. The Scandinavians introduced standard-sized packaging for timber. Both the containers and the packaged timber required totally different types of ship. These were vessels with large hatch-openings and a minimum of wasted hold space. Oskar Wehr responded to the challenge at once.

A long-standing friend from Delfzijl was instru-

keinem Unterstau. Die Reederei Oskar Wehr KG trug der neuen Entwicklung unverzüglich Rechnung. Zum Neubau JANNE WEHR kam Wehr durch einen langjährigen Freund in Delfzijl. Sietas war Mitte der sechziger Jahre, wie die anderen Werften auch, gut ausgelastet und preislich nicht flexibel. Seinem holländischen Freund nannte Wehr die Kriterien, die sein Neubau erfüllen müßte: Rheingängigkeit, eine Luke, mindestens Stauplatz für 63 Container des 20-Fuß-Typs, zwei moderne Ladebäume und eine gutes Intake für die Holzfahrt. Der deutsche Schiffbauingenieur Vogel entwickelte ein solches Schiff nach diesen Spezifikationen, aber die Werft wollte für ein einziges Schiff nicht die hohen Entwicklungskosten übernehmen und forderte mindestens eine Dreier-Serie. „Darf ich mir erlauben, mich über Ihre Vermögensverhältnisse zu erkundigen?", fragte der Werftdirektor, und Oskar Wehr unterschrieb eine entsprechende Genehmigung. Die Auskunft der Commerzbank in Leer war sehr positiv, Oskar Wehr unterzeichnete einen Auftrag über einen 420/890 BRT-Freidecker mit zwei Optionen. Den Preis hatte er auf 1,8 Millionen DM senken können. Ein vergleichbares Schiff hätte in Deutschland etwa 400.000 DM mehr gekostet, auch wenn man berücksichtigt, daß der holländische Bau in einigen Kleinigkeiten nicht ganz so hochwertig wie etwa ein Sietasbau war.

Eines Tages klopfte ihm der niederländische Freund auf die Schulter und sagte: „Du, ich bin Deine erste Option schon losgeworden, Du kriegst 50.000 Gulden von mir!" Das wollte Oskar Wehr eigentlich gar nicht und handelte die Abfindung auf das Doppelte hoch. Zudem bestand er darauf, über die zweite Option allein verfügen zu können. Das konnte er, und verdiente mit der Rückgabe der Option an die

mental in persuading Wehr to place the order for his next new ship, the JANNE WEHR. Like other shipyards in the mid-'sixties, Sietas was booked out, and not all that flexible on the subject of prices. Wehr told his Dutch friend what criteria his new ship would have to fulfil: Rhine/seagoing capabilities, one hold, stowage capacity for a minimum of 63 containers of the 20' type, two modern cargo derricks and good intake facilities for timber. German naval architect Vogel duly designed a ship which complied with these specifications, but the yard was not prepared to bear the full development costs for a single vessel and stipulated a minimum series of three sister ships. "May I make enquiries as to your financial standing?" the yard manager asked, and Oskar Wehr agreed in writing. The information supplied by Commerzbank in Leer must have been more than satisfactory, as Oskar Wehr signed a contract for one 420/890-GRT open shelter-decker, with two further options. He had negotiated the price down to DM 1.8 million, about DM 400,000 less than a comparable ship would have cost in Germany. This was in spite of the fact that in some minor aspects the new Dutch ship were not of the same high quality as a ship built by Sietas.

One day his Dutch friend patted Oskar Wehr on the back and said: "I was able to settled your first option. Now I owe you 50,000 Guilders." This was not what Oskar Wehr had had in mind and he pushed the sum up to double the amount. He also insisted on having exclusive rights for the second option. These he used and made a respectable profit when he eventually waived the option in favour of the yard. In those days shipyards were glad when they could pass on an order. The JANNE WEHR was a good ship. She was given the owner's elder daughter's

Kiellegung für die JANNE WEHR (1) in Bergum und der Stapellauf am 6.9.1968.

Laying the keel for mv JANNE WEHR (1) at Bergum; Launching on 6.9.1968.

Werft nicht schlecht. Das waren noch Zeiten, als die Werften sich freuten, einen Auftrag wieder loszuwerden! JANNE WEHR, so benannt nach dem Rufnamen der älteren Tochter – nach dem Untergang der MARIANNE WEHR mochte die Familie den Namen nicht mehr vergeben – war ein gutes Schiff. Die Idee der Gemeinschaftsmesse erwies sich in der Praxis als nicht so glücklich, als Holzfahrer war das Schiff ein voller Erfolg. Mit seinem Sechs-Zylinder-MWM-Motor lief der Frachter schneller als ähnliche Typen von Sietas. Sechs Jahre später erwarb ein griechischer Reeder das Schiff für 2,8 Millionen DM.

1970 hatte die Reederei die JÜRGEN WEHR (1) an eine von Adolf Feindt betreute Vermögensgesellschaft verkauft, HUGO SELMER fand 1973 neue italienische Eigner und JANNE WEHR (1) war nach Griechenland verkauft worden. Bereits 1968 bekam Jos. L. Meyer den Auftrag, ein rund 5000 tdw großes Semi-Containerschiff zu bauen. Weil die Papenburger Werft einen attraktiven Fährschiffneubau für die schwedische Rederi A/B Slite (die 1993 den Fährschiffsjumbo EUROPA nicht abnehmen konnte) 'dazwischen' bekam, verzögerte sich die Ablieferung auf den 20. September 1970. Das war nicht so schlimm, weil der Markt zum ursprünglichen Termin Mitte 1969 ohnehin eine Schwäche zeigte, und die Werft eine beträchtliche Konventionalstrafe bezahlte. Der Frachter wurde zwar auf den Namen PETER WEHR nach dem Vater des Reeders getauft, in Fahrt kam er als HARTFORD EXPRESS (nach einer Hafenstadt in Neu England) auf Wunsch des langfristigen Zeitcharterers New England Express Line, einer Atlantik Container Line, die sich lange, aber nicht ewig halten konnte. Die ursprüngliche Absicht, noch ein Schwesterschiff zu or-

nickname. The family did not want to use the name Marianne again after the loss of the MARIANNE WEHR. The new ship proved successful in the timber trade but the idea of having a common mess room was less successful. With her six-cylinder MWM engine she was faster than similar types of Sietas' ships. She was bought by a Greek owner for DM 2.8 million six years later.

In 1970 the JÜRGEN WEHR (1) was sold to a financial company managed by Adolf Feindt. The HUGO SELMER went to new Italian owners in 1973 and the JANNE WEHR found a Greek owner. Wehr had already placed an order in 1968 with Jos. L. Meyer for a semi-container vessel of about 5,000 tdw to be built. Delivery did not take place until 20th September 1970, as the Papenburg shipyard had to fit in an order for a new ferry for the Swedish Rederi A/B Slite, who as owners had been unable to take delivery of the jumbo ferry EUROPA in 1993. Wehr did not particularly mind, as the market had begun to weaken at the time (mid-1969) and the yard had to pay a high compensatory fee. The ship was called the PETER WEHR, after the owner's father, but was taken into commission as the HARTFORD EXPRESS. The name had been requested by her long-term time charterers, the New England Express Line, a trans-Atlantic container line which managed to survive for a long time but not for ever. Wehr dropped his original idea of ordering a sister ship, due to the delays in the first new ship, which had caused funds to be blocked. Payment had to be in four instalments, which forced his plans for development to take a completely different turn. The yard subsequently built two similar ships for the Weser Schiffahrtsagentur, but strictly speaking the HARTFORD EXPRESS remained a unique ship.

JANNE WEHR (1) auf Gästefahrt.
Helga, Oskar und Gabriele Wehr (Mitte) und das Ehepaar Helga und Werner Schultz beim Stapellauf der PETER WEHR (1) am 21.8.1970 in Papenburg.

mv JANNE WEHR (1) on her handing-over trip (above); (therebelow:) Helga, Oskar, Gabriele Wehr; (bottom:) Mr and Mrs Werner and Helga Schultz at the launching, at Papenburg on 21.8.1970, of mv PETER WEHR (1).

dern, wurde fallengelassen, weil die Entwicklung durch die Verzögerung des ersten Neubaus und dadurch blockierte Gelder (zu zahlen war in vier Raten) einen anderen als den geplanten Verlauf genommen hatte. Für die Weser Schiffahrtsagentur entstanden zwei ähnliche Nachbauten, genau genommen blieb HARTFORD EXPRESS jedoch ein Einzelschiff.

Motorschiff HARTFORD EXPRESS (1).   *mv HARTFORD EXPRESS (1).*

Das erste Schiff mit der optimalen Brücke

Knappe zwei Jahre später bestellte Oskar Wehr bei Johann Jacob Sietas ein modernes Freidecker-Kümo. Einen verhandlungsbereiteren Sietas hatte er nie zuvor und nie mehr hinterher kennengelernt. JÜRGEN WEHR (2) basierte auf dem Typ 72, von dem Sietas zuvor drei Frachter an die Vega-Reederei abgeliefert hatte. Die neue JÜRGEN WEHR (eine Buchstabenfolge, die sich im Rufzeichen des Schiffes wiederfand) war jedoch das erste deutsche Schiff mit einer sogenannten optimalen Brücke. Diese Brücke ermöglichte aufgrund der Anordnung des Fahrpultes und der Bauweise die Bedienung durch einen Mann. Die früher übliche Besetzung einer Brücke mit Wachoffizier und Rudergänger war nicht nötig. Die Personalkosten waren nämlich inzwischen rasant gestiegen und behinderten die Wettbewerbsfähigkeit deutscher Frachter im internationalen Wettbewerb ganz erheblich. Bei der Indienststellung der HELGA WEHR mußte der 2000 Tonner noch mit 17 Mann Besatzung fahren, JÜRGEN WEHR kam mit neun Mann aus und trug 1500 Tonnen. Die deutschen Aufsichtsbehörden machten die Durchsetzung des Fortschrittes nicht eben leicht (man durfte nicht von der *Einmann*-Brücke sprechen), bis auch sie die neue Entwicklung nicht mehr aufhalten konnten. Wie schon einmal beim Bau der GABRIELE WEHR (1) und HELGA WEHR bestellte Oskar Wehr während der Bauphase der JÜRGEN WEHR einen weiteren Neubau, die JANNE WEHR (2). Dieser 999 BRT/2600 tdw-Containerfrachter mit Eisklasse E 3 gehörte zum 83 a, von dem zuvor zwei Schiffe an die Bugsier-, Reederei- und Bergungs-

The first ship with an ultra-modern bridge

Almost two years later Oskar Wehr ordered a modern open shelter-decker coastal ship to be built at the Sietas shipyard. He had never before encountered Sietas as so amenable to negotiation – or was ever to again. The design of the JÜRGEN WEHR (2) was based on the Sietas' Type 72. The yard had just completed three ships of that type for the Vega-Reederei. The new JÜRGEN WEHR (whose initials were used to make up the call sign of the ship, DNJW) was the first German ship to have an ultra-modern bridge. With an optimum construction and instrumental layout, it was designed for one-man operation instead of the customary officer plus helmsman. By then personnel costs had soared, which began to affect the competitiveness of German freighters on the international market. When the 2,000-tonne HELGA WEHR was taken into commission she had had a crew of 17. The JÜRGEN WEHR, with her 1,500-tonne capacity, managed on seven. The German authorities did not exactly make the process towards modernization easy (and did not permit the expression 'one-man bridge') but were ultimately unable to stop the new trend. As he had already done before during the construction of the GABRIELE WEHR (1) and the HELGA WEHR, Oskar Wehr ordered another new ship while the JÜRGEN WEHR was still under construction, the JANNE WEHR (2). She was a 999-GRT/2,600 tdw container vessel with E3 Ice Classification, of the 83a Type. Two ships of the same type had already been delivered to the Bugsier-, Reederei-

JÜRGEN WEHR (2) vor der Verlängerung.

mv JÜRGEN WEHR (2) prior to jumboising.

AG, eines an D. Tamke und das Typschiff SAGITTA an Peter Döhle geliefert worden waren. Weitere, tiefer gehende und damit mehr tragende Varianten wurden für Döhle und Hermann Wulff gebaut.

Der geplante Bau eines 11.000 tdw-Singledeckers wurde 1976 kurz vor dem Verhandlungsabschluß wieder aufgegeben, weil man letztendlich die hauseigene 'Größe' damals doch nicht so erheblich ausweiten wollte, und ein veränderter Markt nicht die erhofften Erlöse in Aussicht stellte. Das Schiff sollte zu einer Dreierserie von Ujina Shipbuilding gehören. Eine andere deutsche Reederei übernahm dann statt einem zwei Kontrakte, diese Reederei war in der Schiffsgröße zu Hause. Schon einige Jahre zuvor hatte Oskar Wehr mit einer Werft in Belgrad die Aufträge zum Bau von drei kleineren Freideckern weit vorangetrieben, aber die gewünschte Absicherung zu zahlender Bauraten war nicht zu erzielen.

und Bergungs-AG and one to D. Tamke. Peter Döhle had taken delivery of another, the SAGITTA. Other deeper-draught – and therefore higher capacity – vessels had also been built for Döhle and Hermann Wulff.

In 1976, shortly before negotiations were concluded, the plan to build a 11,000-tdw single-decker was scrapped, mainly because Oskar Wehr did not wish to deviate from the size of ship the company already had, as the prospects offered by a change in market were not as promising as they might have been. The ship was to be one of a series of three for Ujina Shipbuilding. Another German shipping company, one used to ships of that size, took on two orders instead of one. A few years before that Oskar Wehr had pressed negotiations with a Belgrade shipyard for three small open shelter-decker but had not been able to get coverage for the instalment payments at the time.

JANNE WEHR (2) auf der Übergabefahrt am 14.6.1974 und im Nord-Ostsee-Kanal (unten).

mv JANNE WEHR (2) on her handing-over trip on 14.6.1974 and in Kiel Canal (below).

Diversifizierung mit neuen Schiffstypen

1975/76 zählte die deutschen Küstenschiffsflotte zu den modernsten der Welt. Insbesondere Küstenschiffsreeder hatten die Entwicklung der Containerschiffe innovativ mitgestaltet. Die Flotte der Reederei Oskar Wehr KG bestand aus fünf modernen Schiffen mit Tragfähigkeiten zwischen 1100 und 5000 Tonnen. 1977 legte sich die Firma mit der Indienststellung des Roll on/Roll off-Schiffes THOMAS WEHR (nach dem ersten Enkelkind) neben der traditionellen Küsten- und der Containerfahrt noch einen dritten Bereich zu. Die Bremerhavener Rickmers-Werft hatte mit diesem relativ neuen Typ bereits Erfahrungen gesammelt. Oskar Wehr war nach Johann A. Reinecke der zweite deutsche Trampreeder, der ein solches Spezialschiff zum Verchartern auf dem freien Markt betrieb. Die Umstellung der bisherigen Küsten- und anderen Linienstrecken auf Container war noch nicht abgeschlossen, da stellten zukunftsorientierte Linien bereits auf Roll on/Roll off-Frachter um. Frei verfügbare Tonnage war damals sehr knapp. Die Frachter konnten als 1599 BRT-Volldecker mit niedrigen Hafenkosten in der kleinen Fahrt auf Antrag ohne Funker und III. Offizier fahren. Die Heuer des fehlenden III. Offiziers teilten sich jedoch die beiden anderen Offiziere. Die Maschinenanlage ist für den 24stündigen wachfreien Betrieb ausgelegt und kann mit zwei Ingenieuren gefahren werden. Oskar Wehr:

„Aus heutiger Sicht, wo das Problem überfüllter Autobahnen vordringlich ist, kommen die Schiffe in West-Ost und Ost-West-Richtung zu ihrem eigentlichen Zweck, als über See verlängerte

Diversification – new types of ships

In 1975/76 the German coastal shipping fleet was one of the most modern in the world. German coastal shipping companies had been innovative when it came to developing container vessels. The Oskar Wehr KG fleet consisted of five modern ships with deadweight capacities of between 1,100 and 5,000 tonnes. In 1977 the company added a third sphere of activities to those it already had in the coastal and container trade by commissioning the roll on-roll off vessel, the THOMAS WEHR (named after the Wehrs' first grandson). The Rickmers shipyard in Bremerhaven had already had a lot of experience in building this comparatively new type of ship. Oskar Wehr was the second German tramp-ship owner after Johann A. Reinecke to put a specialized vessel of this type up for charter on the open market. Ships on coastal and other regular trade routes had still not converted entirely to containers, so forward-looking shipping companies on regular runs switched to roll on-roll off ships. The amount of tonnage available on the market at the time was small. These freighters were closed shelter-deckers of 1599 GRT, which could operate on short-sea runs, at low port dues and, with special permission, without a Radio Officer or Third Officer. The other two officers divided the Third Mate's salary between them. The ships were equipped with a 24-hour watch-free engine room and only required two engineers.

Oskar Wehr: *"Nowadays, when the problem of too much traffic on motorways is acute, ships which trade in a west-east or east-west direction come into their own. They can use the sea as an extended arm of the motorway and relieve the main roads."*

Autobahn die Landstraßen vom Verkehr zu entlasten."

Die abgeschlossene Zeitcharter für eine zwischen dem Kontinent und Westafrika fahrende Linie erwies sich als großer Erfolg, knapp zwei Jahre fuhr der anfangs für 71 Trailer ausgelegte Neubau als WACRO EXPRESS in diesem Trade. Die ursprünglich 2900 Tonnen tragenden Schiffe sind sowohl für die Kleine als auch die Große Fahrt ausgerüstet, wobei sie aber in der Kleinen Fahrt – anders als bis dato gebaute Schiffe – auch wie Küstenschiffe besetzt werden konnten, was sich in niedrigeren Tageskosten niederschlug.

The time charter which he concluded for a regular shipping route between the continent of Europe and West Africa proved a great success. The new ship, which was originally designed to take 71 trailers, sailed on this trade route for almost two years as the WACRO EXPRESS. The ships originally had a deadweight capacity of 2,900 tonnes and are equipped for both coastal and ocean-going runs – with one difference in comparison to those built up till then: they could be manned as coasters, a fact which obviously affected daily running costs. The Rickmers shipyard then received an order to build a sister ship to the THOMAS WEHR. She was taken into commission on 8th June 1978, as the GABRIELE WEHR.

Der erste Ro/Ro-Neubau THOMAS WEHR kam als WACRO EXPRESS in Fahrt (oben). Stapellauf der GABRIELE WEHR (2) am 14.3.1978 in Bremerhaven, rechts das Ehepaar Arnold und Ingeborg Fölsch.

The first Ro/Ro newbuilding, the mv THOMAS WEHR, commissioned as the WACRO EXPRESS (above); (below:) Launching of mv GABRIELE WEHR (2) at Bremerhaven on 14.3.1978; Mr and Mrs Arnold Fölsch.

GABRIELE WEHR (2) während der Werftprobefahrt.   mv GABRIELE WEHR during yard trial trip.

SIGRID WEHR mit sperrigen Konstruktionsteilen auf der Reise von Wales nach Mittelost (oben) und THOMAS WEHR als TOR NEERLANDIA nach der Verlängerung (unten).

mv SIGRID WEHR on her way from Wales to the Middle East with bulky project cargo (above).
mv TOR NEERLANDIA (ex-THOMAS WEHR) after lengthening (below).

Ein spezielles Spezial-schiff für Schwergut

Bei der Rickmers-Werft gab man einen Nachbau der THOMAS WEHR in Auftrag, der am 8. Juni 1978 als GABRIELE WEHR in Fahrt kam. Bereits 1976 wurde mit der Bestellung des in vieler Hinsicht neuartigen Spezialfrachters SIGRID WEHR (nach der Ehefrau von Jürgen Wehr) ein weiterer Fahrtbereich angestrebt, die Schwergutfahrt. Dieser 2600 tdw-Frachter war auch für die konventionelle Küstenfahrt, speziell für Papier und Holz, wie als Container- oder Trailerfrachter (35 Einheiten) gleichermaßen geeignet. Mit diesem Schiff peilte die Reederei eine Lücke an, die von konventionellen Schwergutfrachtern nicht abgedeckt wurde. Die SIGRID WEHR konnte nämlich auf Grund ihres sehr niedrigen Tiefganges von nur 3,65 m bei voll abgeladenem Schiff (und wann ist ein Schwergutfrachter schon mal auf 'Marke') und ihrer niedrigen Gesamthöhe von nur 12,5 m viele Häfen und Binnenplätze anlaufen, die für normale Seeschiffe unerreichbar sind. Und noch ein Novum hatte dieses Schiff aufzuweisen: langte für sperrige Güter die Raumhöhe von 5,8 m nicht, dann fuhr man eben ohne Lukenabdeckung. Darin unterschied sich dieser Neubau vom Typschiff HELENA HUSMANN. Das Problem des möglicherweise überkommenden Seewassers wurde durch zahllose Speigatten über dem Laderaumboden gelöst, durch die zwar Wasser wieder raus- aber nicht reinfließen konnte. Die Idee zum Bau der SIGRID WEHR war typisch für den stets innovativen Reeder Wehr, der sich gerne Marktnischen suchte, die zwar mehr Engagement kosteten, aber (meist) auch größere Überschüsse brachten.

A special heavy lift carrier

As early as 1976 the company had sought to get a foothold in a new area of activities (the transport of heavy cargo) by ordering a special cargo ship for the purpose. She was named the SIGRID WEHR, after Jürgen Wehr's wife. With her 2,600 tdw, the vessel could carry both conventional cargo in short-sea trading areas, such as paper or timber, or containers or trailers (35 units) as well. Wehr managed to cut a niche for himself with this ship, one which other heavy cargo carriers were unable to fill. The SIGRID WEHR had a very shallow draught of only 3.65 m when full – if heavy lift ships can ever be called full. And as her mean height was only 12.5 m she could call in at many ports and inland harbours which were inaccessible for standard ocean-going ships. The vessel was also equipped with another innovation: when oversized goods exceeded the height of the 5.8 m hold she could still carry them by simply leaving the hatchway open.
This was the difference between the SIGRID WEHR and the HELENA HUSMANN. The problem of seawater entering the hatch was solved by fitting numerous one-way scuppers in the hold, through which water could run out but not run in. The plan to build the SIGRID WEHR was typical of the owner. He had always had innovative ideas and carved his own niches in the market. Even if they entailed a high degree of commitment, on the whole they brought higher returns.
The new vessel, known as a 'deck carrier' in shipping circles, was not a lucky ship. The

Der neue Frachter, der in der Schiffahrt Deckcarrier genannt wurde, stand jedoch unter keinem glücklichen Stern. Mit dem Bau beauftragt hatte Oskar Wehr die Kremer Werft in Elmshorn/Glückstadt. Dieses Unternehmen war nach 143 Jahren Kremer-Regie 1975 in Konkurs geraten. Der Hamburger Unternehmer Ulrich Harms, der sich als Berger einen Namen gemacht hatte, trat als Sanierer auf und übernahm Teile der Werft. Rümpfe von der Größe der SIGRID WEHR mit 100 m Länge konnte die Werft nicht selbst erstellen, sie ließ diese von der Stahlbau-Abteilung der Kieler Howaldtswerke/Deutsche Werft AG bauen. Das klappte auch sehr gut, doch kurz nachdem SIGRID WEHR an die Ausrüstungspier des neuen Kremer-Betriebes in Glückstadt geschleppt wurde, mußte Ulrich Harms eingestehen, daß er die Werft nicht sanieren konnte und im März 1978 erneut Konkurs anmelden mußte. Diese Fehlleistung des Hamburger Unternehmers kostete die Reederei Wehr viel Zeit und Geld. Die Rickmers-Werft in Bremerhaven baute das Schiff zwar zügig fertig, es wies aber statt vereinbarter 3000 Ladetonnen nur etwa 2600 Tonnen auf und war durch den Konkurs auch um einiges teurer geworden.

order to build her had gone to the Kremer Werft in Elmshorn/Glückstadt. After being owned by the Kremer family for 175 years, the yard went bankrupt in 1975. The Hamburg entrepreneur Ulrich Harms, who had made a name for himself in salvaging ships, attempted to rehabilitate the company by taking over various sectors of the shipyard. As the yard was not able to construct hulls a hundred metres long – the size of the SIGRID WEHR's – it had subcontracted the work to the steelworks section of the Howaldtswerke/Deutsche Werft AG in Kiel. This arrangement had worked very well, but by the time the hull of the SIGRID WEHR arrived to be fitted out at the Kremer Werft in Glückstadt, Ulrich Harms admitted he was no longer able to save the yard. Once again, in March 1978, it was declared bankrupt. This misjudgement on Harms' part cost Wehr a great deal of money and time. The Rickmers-Werft in Bremerhaven completed the ship without further delay, but on delivery she was found to have a capacity of only 2,600 tonnes instead of the 3,000 tonnes specified in the contract. The bankruptcy had taken its toll on the final price.

SIGRID WEHR an der Crown Wharf in Rochester.   *mv SIGRID WEHR at the Crown Wharf at Rochester.*

HANSE-FERRIES
WEHR-TRANSPORT GMBH Präsident-Krahn-Straße 18/19, D-2000 Hamburg 50. Tel. (040) 38 17 26/27, Telex 02-12441 OWEHR

BAUJAHR 1978 · DEUTSCHE FLAGGE · 1060 LFD. MTR. STELLFLÄCHE

HAMBURG

BREMEN

Zw
wöch

zu

TRAILER · LASTZÜGE · CONTAINER 20' + 40' · ROLLENDES

CKKLAPPE · 40 TO. LIFT · 6000 PS · 18 KNOTEN · BUGSTRAHLRUDER

al
ntlich
d
ck

SHEERNESS

MIDDLESBROUGH

ALLER ART · NEUFAHRZEUGE · STÜCKGUT AUF ANFRAGE

Eine eigene Firma für die Befrachtung

Nicht zuletzt um dieses fortschrittliche Schiff optimal zu vermarkten, gründete Oskar Wehr Ende 1977 die Wehr Transport GmbH. Mitgesellschafter und Geschäftsführer waren sein Sohn Jürgen sowie der Reedereikaufmann Gert Uwe Detlefsen, der entsprechende Erfahrungen mitbrachte. Diese Firma arbeitete in Bürogemeinschaft mit der Reederei, die inzwischen in der Präsident-Krahn-Straße direkt am Bahnhof Altona ansässig war. Sie agierte fortan als Befrachtungsmakler für die Beschäftigung der Wehrschiffe. Sie arbeitete außerdem erfolgreich im allgemeinen Befrachtungsgeschäft und bildete u.a. die jüngste Tochter des Ehepaars Oskar und Helga Wehr, Gabriele, zur Schifffahrtskauffrau aus. Ein allmählich nachlassender Markt machten die Geschäfte schwieriger, für den modernen Neubau SIGRID WEHR fanden sich trotz intensiver Bemühungen keine entsprechenden Frachtverträge, und in der normalen Holz- und Massengutfahrt konnte das Schiff die nötigen Ergebnisse nicht auffahren. Ein Tonnageüberangebot hatte auch die Raten für Ro/Ro-Frachter drastisch gesenkt und so mußte früher als geplant eine eigene Linie für das jüngere Ro/Ro-Schiff außerhalb des Trampmarktes gefunden werden. Daher hatte die Wehr Transport GmbH 1980 unter dem Namen *Hanse-Ferries* einen Ro-Ro-Liniendienst von Hamburg über Bremen nach Felixstowe und Middlesbrough eröffnet. Zum Einsatz kam die 1599 BRT große GABRIELE WEHR (2), die Platz für 71 Trailer bot. Der Dienst wurde nach einigen Monaten auf die Relation Hamburg-Sheerness konzentriert. Bald erwies

A chartering company of its own

In an attempt to market this ultra-modern ship as best he could, at the end of 1977 Oskar Wehr founded the Wehr Transport GmbH. Co-partners and directors of the company were his son Jürgen and the trained shipping clerk, Gert Uwe Detlefsen, who brought the experience needed with him. The new company worked under the same roof as the shipowners, which had since been re-located at the Präsident-Krahn-Strasse, opposite the railway station in Altona. From then on they became exclusive chartering brokers for the Wehr fleet. The company also carried out successful business as general shipbrokers and Gabriele, Oskar and Helga Wehr's youngest daughter, carried out her training as a shipping clerk with the company. The market was beginning to deteriorate, which made business more difficult and, despite all efforts, no suitable freight contracts could be found for the new ship, and normal timber and bulk trades were not enough to make ends meet. In addition a tonnage glut had sent rates for roll on-roll off ships plummeting, so that Wehr was forced to look for a regular trade route for the youngest ship of this type outside the tramp market, and this much sooner than he had planned.

This is why, under the name of Hanse-Ferries, Wehr Transport GmbH set up a regular roll on-roll off service from Hamburg and Bremen to Felixstowe and Middlesbrough in 1980. With a GRT of 1,599 and a trailer capacity of 71, the GABRIELE WEHR (2) was put on the route. After several months the service was reduced to the Hamburg-Sheerness route. The company's ship soon proved too large. In her

GABRIELE WEHR am Terminal der Hamburger Hafen- und Lagerhaus-Gesellschaft (HHLA) am Burchardkai.

mv GABRIELE WEHR at the Ro/Ro berth of the Burchardkai container terminal of Hamburger Hafen- und Lagerhaus AG (HHLA)

sich das eigene Schiff als zu groß, so daß in diesem Dienst auf Profit/Loss-Sharing zunächst die norwegische PAMELA ex BALDER EEMS (1181 BRT/1770 tdw/1979 Scheepswerf Waterhuizen) aufgenommen wurde. Ohne Notizen oder Kündigung des Vertrages weigerte sich der Kapitän eines Tages nach dem Löschen, neue Ladung zu übernehmen und dampfte davon. Sein Reeder Parley Augusston hatte nun offensichtlich andere Pläne und zog das Schiff aus dem Liniendienst ab. Als Ersatz kam die TRANSIT ex MICHEL (567 BRT/967 tdw/1972 A/S Trondhjems MV) der Reederei Bauer & Hauschildt KG in Hamburg zum Einsatz. Da die beiden Rickmers-Schwestern zu groß und SIGRID WEHR zu langsam für diesen Dienst waren, der aber nur zur Beschäftigung eigener Tonnage aufgenommen worden war, verkaufte man die Linie 1981 an die dänische DFDS, die diesen Dienst seither versieht.

stead, the Norwegian PAMELA, the ex-BALDER EMS (1,181 GRT/1,770 tdw/1979 Scheepswerf Waterhuizen) was put on the route under a profit and loss sharing agreement. After discharging his cargo one day the master flatly refused to take on new cargo, and the ship left port. Allegedly his owner, Parley Augustson, had had other plans and simply withdrew his ship from the run. The TRANSIT, the ex-MICHEL (567 GRT/967 tdw/ 1972 A/S Trondhjems MV), which was owned by Bauer & Hauschildt KG of Hamburg, was then chartered, as both the Rickmers-built sister ships were too large and the SIGRID WEHR too slow for the service. But as the service had only been started in the first place to secure employment for the company's own ships, the line was sold to the Danish company, DFDS, in 1981. They still operate on the same route.

CONTAINERSHIPS I ex JANNE WEHR (2) im winterlichen Hafen von Helsinki (oben). Blick in den Laderaum der JANNE WEHR (2) mit einer Papierladung.

mv CONTAINERSHIPS I ex-JANNE WEHR (2) in the wintry port of Helsinki (above); View of newsprint in the hold of mv JANNE WEHR (2).

Der eigene Liniendienst der Reederei wurde als 'Hanse Ferries' vermarktet.

'Hanse Ferries' was the trade name of the company's own liner service.

TOR ANGLIA ex GABRIELE WEHR (2) und TOR NEERLANDIA ex THOMAS WEHR treffen sich in Rotterdam.

mv TOR ANGLIA ex-GABRIELE WEHR (2) passing mv TOR NEERLANDIA ex-THOMAS WEHR in the port of Rotterdam.

Eine neue 'HELGA WEHR' wurde Flaggschiff

1981/82 vergrößerte die Reederei ihre Tonnage erneut erheblich, ohne daß ein Schiff dazukam. Eine polnische Werft verlängerte JÜRGEN WEHR, JANNE WEHR und SIGRID WEHR, und 1982 fügte die Werft Nobiskrug in Rendsburg den beiden Ro/Ro-Frachtern GABRIELE WEHR und THOMAS WEHR jeweils eine 25-m-Sektion ein, wodurch rund 20 Trailer mehr geladen werden konnten. Parallel dazu hatte die Seebeck Werft AG der AG Weser in Bremerhaven den Auftrag zum Bau eines neuen Flaggschiffes erhalten. Es kam am 24.11.1983 als dritte HELGA WEHR in Fahrt. Der besonders für die Containerfahrt ausgelegte Neubau hat eine BRZ von 13 476 und trägt 19 440 Tonnen. 1152 TEU können gestellt werden, davon 466 unter Deck. Außerdem wurden auf den Decks IV und V einige Kammern für die Mitnahme von Passagieren eingerichtet.

1984, kurz nachdem sich der Reeder seinen Traum vom großen Schiff erfüllen konnte, das er trotz vorhandenen Befähigungszeugnisses nicht fahren will, weil es infolge der Automatisierung 'langweilig' wäre, erlitt Oskar Wehr einen Herzinfarkt, dem 1987 ein zweiter folgte. Inzwischen erhielt er auch eine Ballon Delatation, eine gefährliche Angelegenheit, die glücklicherweise erfolgreich war. Die Belastung durch die Reedereiarbeit war nun zu groß. Es hatte sich daher als positiv ausgewirkt, daß Sohn Jürgen nach langer Zusammenarbeit mit dem Vater die Firma problemlos allein führen konnte. Aus der Wehr Transport GmbH war der geschäftsführende Gesellschafter Gert Uwe Detlefsen mittlerweile ausgeschieden. Die Befrach-

A new 'HELGA WEHR' – a new flag ship

In 1981/82 the Wehr shipping company again expanded its tonnage substantially without the addition of a new ship. The JÜRGEN, the JANNE and the SIGRID WEHR were jumboised at a Polish shipyard. Then in 1982 the roll on-roll off vessels, the GABRIELE and the THOMAS WEHR were each fitted with an additional 25-metre midship section at the Nobiskrug shipyard in Rendsburg, thereby extending their loading capacity by another 20 trailers. At the same time the Seebeck Werft AG in Bremerhaven, an affiliate of the AG Weser, had been contracted to build a new flag ship. The new vessel was taken into commission on 24th November 1983 – the third HELGA WEHR. She was built as a container ship and, with a gross tonnage of 13,476, was capable of carrying 19,440 tonnes. She could accommodate 1,152 TEU in containers, 466 below deck, and had passenger cabins on Decks IV and V.

Wehr's dream of owning a large ship had been realised, although, in spite of holding the appropriate license, he never considered taking over its command, as he thought the job would have become boring after automation. In 1984, shortly after taking delivery of the ship, he had a heart attack, followed by a second in 1987. He underwent angioplasty surgery, a dangerous operation, but fortunately proved successful. The burden of work in the office had taken its toll. The fact that Jürgen Wehr worked alongside his father for a long time and was capable of managing it on his own, without any bother, now had its

1993/4 fuhr HELGA WEHR (2) als CMB ENERGY (oben) und 1985 als MAERSK CLAUDINE (unten).

mv HELGA WEHR traded as the CMB ENERGY in 1993/94 (above) and as the MAERSK CLAUDINE in 1985 (below)

tungsabteilung war 1984 mit Eckhard Nemitz neu besetzt worden, sie ist inzwischen als S & C Wehr Transport GmbH (S und C stehen für Shipping und Chartering) erfolgreich im Vermitteln von Fracht- und Schiffahrtsgeschäften auf dem internationalen Markt tätig und sie konzentriert sich vor allem auf weltweite Containerbefrachtung.

Für das 'Sorgenkind' SIGRID WEHR fand sich 1989 in Norwegen ein neuer Eigner. Inzwischen ist das Schiff im iranischen Bandar Abbas beheimatet. Die Befrachtung der kleineren Frachter liegt jetzt in den Händen der Hamburger Maklerfirma Meerpahl & Meyer GmbH, deren Inhaber mit Jürgen Wehr schon seit alten Transmar-Zeiten zusammenarbeiteten. Meerpahl & Meyer sahen sich 1989 plötzlich in einer ungewohnten Position. Sie hatten gute Ladungsverbindungen, nach dem Weggang eines Prinzipals aber zu wenig Schiffe in der 3000 tdw-Klasse. Um die Lücke zu füllen, erwarb Jürgen Wehr auf dem Gebrauchtmarkt drei 3000 tdw-Singledecker, die 1977/78 in den Niederlanden gebaut wurden. Während diese Schiffe für Antigua-Tochtergesellschaften als CAROLINE, CHRISTINA und SIGRID ohne den üblichen Familiennamen in Fahrt kamen, erhielt ein etwas später angekaufter 3000-tdw-Sietasbau den Namen BIRTE WEHR nach der ersten Reederstochter, da er zunächst unter deutscher Flagge blieb. Bei der Finanzierung wählte Jürgen Wehr erstmals in der Reedereigeschichte das Modell von Kapitalgesellschaften mit mehreren Investoren. Sein Vater hatte die ersten Schiffe allein finanziert und bei den späteren Neubauten arbeitete er mit den Partnern Arnold Fölsch und dem Ehepaar Schultz zusammen,

positive effects.

In the meantime the managing partner in Wehr Transport GmbH, Gert Uwe Detlefsen, left the company and Eckhard Nemitz assumed his position when he took over the chartering section in 1984. The company has since been successful as international shipping and chartering brokers under the name of Wehr Transport GmbH & Co. KG, specializing in container transport worldwide.

The SIGRID WEHR still remained a problem child, but she found a new owner in Norway in 1989. Her brokers were still the Hamburg company, Meerpahl & Meyer GmbH, whose proprietors have been working with Jürgen Wehr since their time together at Transmar. Meerpahl & Meyer suddenly found themselves in a curious position in 1989. They had excellent connections where cargo was concerned but, after losing one of their principals, lacked ships of 3,000 tdw size. To fill the gap, Jürgen Wehr bought three singledeckers of 3,000 tdw second-hand. and Built in the Netherlands in 1977/78 and commissioned for an Antiguan subsidiary, the ships entered service as the CAROLINE, the CHRISTINA and the SIGRID (without the customary family surname). Another 3,000 tonne Sietas-built ship with German flag, bought second-hand, was also taken into operation as the BIRTE WEHR, named after Jürgen's eldest daughter. For the first time in the history of the company Jürgen Wehr financed his purchases through proprietary companies with several investors. His father had financed his first ships on his own and, when purchasing new ships, later worked together with his partners Arnold Fölsch and the

HELGA WEHR (3) und TOR ANGLIA ex HELGA WEHR (2) treffen sich auf dem Nieuwe Waterweg bei Rotterdam.

mv HELGA WEHR (3) and mv TOR ANGLIA ex-GABRIELE WEHR (2) passing each other on the Nieuwe Waterweg near Rotterdam.

die sich immer im gleichen Minderheitsverhältnis an den Wehrschiffen beteiligten.

Die CHRISTINA sank nach nur einjähriger Fahrtzeit nach einer Kollision mit dem schwedischen Tanker EK CLOUD auf der Weser, wobei Personenschaden glücklicherweise nicht zu verzeichnen war. Nach der Bergung stellten sich die Schäden als so schwerwiegend heraus, daß die Versicherung die Havarie als Totalschaden abrechnete. Ende 1993 wurden die beiden verbliebenen Singledecker dieses Trios ebenfalls verkauft.

Anfang 1992 zog die Reederei um. Die Räume in der Präsident-Krahn-Straße mit Blick auf den Altonaer Bahnhof wurden vom Hauseigentümer selbst benötigt. In Schenefeld, unmittelbar an der Grenze Hamburgs zu Schleswig-Holstein konnte ein nagelneues Bürohaus erworben werden. In der Blankeneser Chaussee

Schultzes, who had equal minority shares in his ships.

The CHRISTINA sank after only one year in service, following a collision with a Swedish tanker, the EK CLOUD, on the River Weser. Fortunately there were no casualties. After being salvaged, she was found to have incurred such heavy damage that the insurance company declared her a total loss. The other two single-deckers which made up the trio were sold at the end of 1993.

Early in 1992 the shipping company once again moved offices, as the owner of the premises in the Präsident-Krahn-Strasse, opposite Altona station, required them for his own use. Wehr bought a brand new office building in Schenefeld, No. 181, Blankeneser Chaussee, on the border between Hamburg and Schleswig-Holstein.

Den gelben 'Rallystreifen' am Vorschiff führen inzwischen alle Wehr-Schiffe. Hier BIRTE WEHR. Einige Jahre lang nahm die HELGA WEHR (3) auch Passagiere mit.

All Wehr vessels now wear the yellow 'rally streak' as seen here on the BIRTE WEHR (above); mv HELGA WEHR (3) offered passenger accommodation for a few years (below).

IMKE WEHR (oben) und PETER WEHR (2) fahren vorwiegend in fernöstlichen Gewässern.

mv IMKE WEHR (above) and mv PETER WEHR (2) mainly trade in the Far East.

181 in Schenefeld sind die Reederei Oskar Wehr KG (GmbH & Co) und die S & C Wehr Transport GmbH mit ihren insgesamt rund ein Dutzend Angestellten tätig. Prokuristen der Reederei sind Reinhold Meyer, Chef der Buchhaltung, und Dieter Grundmann, Leiter der Inspektionsabteilung.

Im Juli 1992 kaufte Jürgen Wehr für wiederum zwei in St. John's, Antigua and Barbuda angesiedelte Tochtergesellschaften die beiden Containerschiffe JOHANNGEORGENSTADT und JÖHSTADT. Die beiden je 7740 tdw großen, für 440 TEU ausgerüsteten Schiffe gehören zum Typ VCS 420 (Vollcontainerschiff für 420 TEU), den die damals noch staatseigene Deutsche Seereederei 1984/6 in Spanien bauen ließ. Während der erste Frachter als IMKE WEHR (nach der zweiten Reederstochter) übernommen wurde, erhielt die JÖHSTADT aufgrund einer Zeitcharter den Namen KHYBER, fährt aber seit 1993 unter dem vorgesehenen Namen PETER WEHR (2). Beide Schiffe wurden nach der Übernahme umgebaut und die Containerkapazität auf 580 TEU erhöht. Später wurden auch die Hauptmotoren modernisert, so daß beide Schiffe jetzt jeweils 16 Knoten laufen.

Im Sommer 1993 bestellte die Reederei bei der inzwischen privatisierten und zum Verbund des Bremer Vulkans gehörenden MTW Schiffswerft GmbH in Wismar zwei Vollcontainerschiffe des Typs CC 1600 mit rund 22.200 tdw und 1618 Containerstellplätzen (TEU). Kurz darauf konnte die JÜRGEN WEHR (2) nach zwanzigjähriger Fahrtzeit unter der Wehrflagge nach Dänemark verkauft werden, wo der Umbau in einen Säuretanker geplant war. Das Segment Küstenschiffahrt ist seither nur mit der BIRTE WEHR besetzt.

In July 1992 Jürgen Wehr again bought two container vessels for two subsidiaries which were registered in St. John's/Antigua and in Barbuda, the JOHANNGEORGENSTADT and the JÖHSTADT. Each of the ships could carry 7,740 tdw and had a capacity for 440 TEU. They were built in Spain in 1984/86 for the then state-owned Deutsche Seereederei and were of the VCS 420 type (full container ships, 420 TEU). The first ship was named the IMKE WEHR, after the owner's second daughter, while the JÖHSTADT was named the KHYBER when she was taken into time charter. In 1993 she was renamed the PETER WEHR (2) again, the name originally intended for her. Both ships were rebuilt after being taken into service by the company resulting in a new container capacity of 580 TEU. Their main engines were also modernized, increasing their speed to 16 knots.

In the summer of 1993 the company placed an order for two full container ships of the CC 1600 type (each with around 22,200 tdw and a container capacity of 1,618 TEU) with the MTW Schiffswerft GmbH in Wismar. The shipyard has since been privatised and become part of the Bremer Vulkan group. Shortly after, following twenty years of service under Wehr, the JÜRGEN WEHR (2) was sold to a Danish company, which had plans to convert her into an acid tanker. Several years later, the BIRTE WEHR, the only remaining coastal ship in the company, was sold.

Singledecker SIGRID vor Cuxhaven (oben) und CAROLINE an der Husumer Werft.

Singledeck mv SIGRID of Cuxhaven (above) and mv CAROLINE alongside Husumer Werft shipyard.

Oskar Wehr am 24.11.1983 an Bord HELGA WEHR (3) (links). Jürgen Wehr 1994 (rechts).
In Schenefeld unmittelbar an der Hamburger Stadtgrenze ist die Reederei Oskar Wehr KG (GmbH & Co) seit 1991 ansässig, mit der Wehr Familie (unten), vlnr Thomas, Sigrid, Jürgen, Imke und Birte Wehr.

Oskar Wehr on board the HELGA WEHR (3) on 24.11.1983 (left), Jürgen Wehr in 1994 (right).
Seat of Oskar Wehr KG (GmbH & Co) since 1991, in Schenefeld immediately adjacent to the border of the city of Hamburg, with the Wehr familiy (below), from left: Thomas, Sigrid, Jürgen, Imke and Birte Wehr.

Containerschiffsneubau aus Polen

Die beiden MTW-Neubauten konnten Anfang 1994 an von der Leeraner Reederei Hermann Buss & Cie. betreute Eigentumsgesellschaften verkauft werden. Im Herbst 1995 stieg die Reederei Wehr in den Bauvertrag für einen 1170-TEU-Containerfrachter vom Typ B 190 ein, den die zypriotische Schoeller Holdings Ltd. bei der Stocznia Szczecinska SA in Stettin zur Lieferung zum Jahresende 1995 im Rahmen einer Sechserserie unterzeichnet hatte. Für diesen Neubau übernahm das im Sommer 1995 von den Reedereien Ernst Komrowski, Ernst Russ, Oskar Wehr sowie dem An- und Verkaufsmakler Andreas J. Zachariassen gegründete Emissionshaus Lloyd Fonds Gesellschaft für Schiffs- und Immobilienbeteiligungen mbH & Co., Hamburg, die Plazierung auf dem Kapitalmarkt und gab damit ihr Emissionsdebüt.

Der am 29.12.1995 abgelieferte Neubau SIGRID WEHR (2) trat unverzüglich nach Infahrtsetzung eine längerfristige Zeitcharter bei der zur Toepfer-Gruppe gehörenden Independent Container Line im Rahmen deren Liniendienstes von Antwerpen in die US-Häfen Richmond und Philadelphia als INDEPENDENT VENTURE an. Nach deren Ende wurde der Frachter in Hamburg mit zwei 40 Tonnen-Kranen ausgerüstet und in eine neue Charter angeliefert.

Kurz vor der Übernahme des 13.700-Tonners SIGRID WEHR hatte Jürgen Wehr zur Lieferung in 1997 zwei weitere Baukontrakte übernommen. Es handelte sich diesmal wiederum um zwei Containerschiffe von der Stocznia

New container ships from Poland

Early in 1994 the two newly-built MTW ships were sold to ownership companies managed by the Hermann Buss & Cie. shipping company in Leer. In the autumn of 1995 Oskar Wehr KG entered into a building contract for a 1,170 TEU containership of the B 190 type, which the Cypriot company, Schoeller Holdings Ltd. in Limassol, had originally contracted with the Stocznia Szczecinska SA shipyard in Stettin, as one of a series of six ships to be delivered at the end of 1995. In the summer of 1995 an underwriting business was set up in Hamburg by the shipowners Ernst Komrowski, Ernst Russ, Oskar Wehr, and the sales and purchasing brokers Andreas J. Zachariassen, for funding of the new ships. The firm was called "Lloyd Fonds Gesellschaft für Schiffs- und Immobilienbeteiligungen mbH & Co." and with this project made its debut as an underwriting company on the ship financing market.

The SIGRID WEHR (2) was completed on 29th December 1995 and delivered as the INDEPENDENT VENTURE for time charter with the Independent Container Line, part of the Toepfer Group. Here she joined the line's regular service between Antwerp and the US ports of Richmond and Philadelphia. After completion of this contract, the ship was fitted out with two 40-tonne deck cranes in Hamburg and continued trading under another charter party.

Shortly before taking delivery of the 13,700-tdw SIGRID WEHR, Jürgen Wehr assumed control of two more new building contracts for

SIGRID WEHR (2) als INDEPENDENT VENTURE in Charter der Independent Container Line auslaufend auf der Schelde. Und SIGRID WEHR (2) als Containerschiff mit Geschirr und einer vollen Ladung neuer Leercontainer.

SIGRID WEHR (2) as INDEPENDENT VENTURE under charter of Independent Container Line leaving River Scheldt. And SIGRID WEHR (2) as geared containership with a full cargo of brand new empty boxes.

Containership CSAV RIO DE LA PLATA ex- WEHR ALTONA.

Szczecinska, aber vom größeren Typ B 170, die ursprünglich von der chilenischen Reederei CSAV Compania Sud Americana de Vapores, Valparaiso, bestellt wurden. Diese Reederei nahm die beiden Frachter im Rahmen der Transaktion für zwei Jahre in Zeitcharter. Im 14-Tages-Abstand am 19. September bzw. 2. Oktober 1997 wurden sie als WEHR ALTONA und WEHR OTTENSEN abgeliefert und gingen unmittelbar darauf als CSAV RIO DE LA PLATA und CSAV RIO GRANDE in Charter.

delivery in 1997. Once again these were for container ships to be supplied by the Stocznia Szczecinska, but of a larger size (B 170), orders for which had originally been placed by the Chilean shipping company CSAV, Compañia Sud Americana de Vapores, of Valparaiso. CSAV then took both vessels into time charter for two years as a part of the deal. The ships were both delivered within a fortnight – on the 19th September and 2nd October 1997 – as the WEHR ALTONA and the WEHR OTTENSEN, whereupon they assumed their chartered names – CSAV RIO DE LA PLATA and CSAV RIO GRANDE.

Containership KOTA SEJARAH ex- WEHR ALTONA.

Zuvor war dieses Duo um zwei weitere B 170-Frachter auf ein Quartett erweitert worden. Diese beiden Schiffe wurden am 11. Februar bzw. 26. März 1998 als WEHR KOBLENZ und WEHR MÜDEN von der Stettiner Werft an die Reederei abgeliefert. Im kleinen Moselort Müden wuchs der Firmengründer Oskar Wehr auf, in Koblenz kam er zur Welt. Die Charternamen lauten CSAV RIO AMAZONAS und CSAV RIMAC.

Drei Neubauten begannen ihre Jungfernreisen nach der Überführungsfahrt von Stettin durch den Nord-Ostseekanal in ihrem Heimathafen Hamburg. Die chilenische Linienreederei beschäftigte diese Einheiten in ihrem mit fünf Schiffen der 1500/1700 TEU-Klasse betriebenen Dienst mit Abfahrten alle neun Tage vom Kontinent (Felixstowe, Rotterdam, Hamburg, Antwerpen, Le Havre und Bilbao) nach Rio de Janeiro, Santos, Paranagua, Itajai, Rio Grande, Montevideo, Buenos Aires und zurück.

Im Herbst 1998 erweiterte die Reederei Wehr ihre vier Typ B 170-Frachter um zwei weitere dieser international bewährten und universell einsetzbaren Containerschiffe. Sie wurden von der chilenischen Compania Chilena de Navegacion Interoceanica SA, Valparaiso, in längerfristige Zeitcharter genommen und kamen im Sommer 1999 in Fahrt. Sie liefen am 10. April bzw. 5. Mai 1999 als WEHR FLOTTBEK und WEHR RISSEN vom Stapel.

Shortly before, the previous order for two ships was doubled to four ships of the type B170. The two additional ships from Stettin were delivered to the Wehr shipping company on 11th February and 26th March 1998 as the WEHR KOBLENZ and the WEHR MÜDEN (the names being of significance to Oskar Wehr, the founder of the company, who was born in Koblenz and grew up in the village of Müden on the river Moselle.) Once under charter the ships were renamed CSAV RIO AMAZONAS and CSAV RIMAC.

Following their transfer from Stettin through the Kiel Canal, three of the new ships commenced their maiden voyages from their home port of Hamburg. The Chilean shipping line operated the four ships on their regular route with altogether five 1,500/1,700-TEU container vessels between the European continental ports of Felixstowe, Rotterdam, Hamburg, Antwerp, Le Havre and Bilbao to Rio de Janeiro, Santos, Paranagua, Itajai, Rio Grande, Montevideo and Buenos Aires, Montevideo, Rio Grande, Montevideo, Buenos Aires.

By the autumn of 1998 the Wehr shipping company due to the ship's good international standing and versatility added a further two ships of the type B 170 to their existing fleet of four ships. These new ships were then taken under long-term charter by the Chilean company Chilena de Navegacion Interoceanica SA of Valparaiso. They were launched as the WEHR FLOTTBEK and the WEHR RISSEN on the 10th April and 5th May 1999 and began trading in the summer of 1999.

Containerschiff CSAV RIMAC ex WEHR MÜDEN auf der Reise von der Bauwerft nach Hamburg.

Containership CSAV RIMAC ex- WEHR MÜDEN on her voyage from the builders to Hamburg.

Containerschiff WEHR FLOTTBEK.

Ein schwerer Verlust für Familie und Reederei

Am 24. Juni 1998 verstarb der Firmengründer, Kapitän und Reeder Oskar Wehr, im 78. Lebensjahr. Eine große Zahl von Familienangehörigen, angeführt von der Witwe Helga Wehr, den Töchtern Marianne und Gabriele sowie Sohn Jürgen mit Ehepartnern, sieben Enkelkindern, Mitarbeitern von Land und Seeleuten, Freunden und Geschäftspartnern gaben ihm am 1. Juli 1998 auf dem Hamburger Friedhof Nienstedten in unmittelbarer Nähe der Elbe das letzte Geleit.

Die Familie und die Schiffahrtszene verlor mit Oskar Wehr einen erfahrenen Praktiker, der sich trotz des starken Engagements für das eigene Unternehmen auch für zahlreiche Ehrenämter zur Verfügung gestellt hatte, und der sich mit der Umsetzung von Innovationen in der eigenen Flotte dem Strukturwandel in der Seeschiffahrt immer rechtzeitig angepaßt hat. Seine Sachkenntnis und sein trockener Humor werden nicht nur seiner Familie und Freunden fehlen.

An acute loss for family and company

The founder of the company, Master Mariner and shipowner Oskar Wehr, died on the 24th June 1998, aged 77. Many members of the family assembled to pay their respects to him on 1st July at the Nienstedten cemetery, close to the banks of the River Elbe. They were led by his widow Helga Wehr, his daughters Marianne and Gabriele and their husbands, his son Jürgen and his wife, seven grandchildren, shore-based and shipping staff, personal friends and business partners.

Oskar Wehr had accumulated significant practical experience in shipping and his loss was acutely felt by both family and the shipping sector as a whole. He was dedicated to his company but nonetheless still found time to participate in numerous honorary positions. He remained on the cutting edge of technology, implementing new innovations in response to market situations. His expertise and dry sense of humour will be missed not only by his family and friends.

Generations- und Ortswechsel

Jürgen Wehr, die Mitarbeiter an Land und auf See, führen die Reederei Oskar Wehr KG (GmbH & Co.) im Geiste des Gründers fort. Das eigene Bürohaus in Schenefeld, unmittelbar an dem die Stadtgrenze zu Hamburg, markierenden Ortsschild, konnte das durch die größere Flotte gewachsene Büropersonal nicht mehr angemessen unterbringen. Die eigenen Räume wurden vermietet, und zum 1. April 1999 bezog die Reederei Oskar Wehr KG (GmbH & Co.) sowie die Maklerfirma Wehr Transport GmbH & Co. KG direkt neben der Hamburg-Süd an der Ost-West-Straße neue, großzügig dimensionierte Büroräume. Die sich

A new generation, new address

Jürgen Wehr and his company staff continue to run the Oskar Wehr (GmbH & Co.) in the spirit in which it was founded, both on land and on board. The office in Schenefeld (next to the sign marking the City boundary) gradually became too small to accommodate the number of office staff needed to accommodate the expanding fleet, so the former premises were leased out and, on 1st April 1999, the Oskar Wehr (GmbH & Co.) and the shipbroking company Wehr Transport GmbH & Co. KG moved to new, spacious premises located at Ost-West-Strasse 61. The modern offices, which occupy two stories of the build-

Die Büro-Mannschaft der Reederei Wehr im Empfangsbereich des Büros.

Oskar Wehrs office staff behind the reception desk.

über zwei Stockwerke erstreckenden Räume wurden nach ergonomischen Erkenntnissen ausgestattet. Die lichtdurchfluteten Büros sind klimatisiert, alle Arbeitsplätze wurden mit moderner Kommunikations- und Datenverarbeitungstechnik ausgerüstet und vernetzt.

Auf die umfassende Qualifikation der Mitarbeiter, deren Zahl analog zur wachsenden Flotte stieg, legt der Reedereinhaber größten Wert. Die Qualifikation der Mitarbeiter ist in jedem Unternehmen eine wesentliche Voraussetzung für Zuverlässigkeit und Leistung, für Dienstleistungsunternehmen wie die Reederei Oskar Wehr KG (GmbH & Co.) ist dies von besonderer Bedeutung. Moderne Tonnage auf See; modernes Büro an Land: beides ist ohne Menschen, die mit den technischen Ausrüstungen nicht perfekt und zuverlässig umgehen können, wertlos. Die Förderung der Aus- und Weiterbildung der Mitarbeiter ist ein wichtiger Baustein in der Personalpolitik der Reederei. Bei Erscheinen dieses Buches befinden sich zwei junge Damen und zwei junge Herren in der Ausbildung zum Schiffahrtskauffrau/-mann. Sprachlehrgänge, Fortbildungsseminare und derzeit ein Praxissemester für einen Studenten der Betriebswirtschaftslehre stehen auf dem Förderungsprogramm der Reederei.

Eine große Anforderung an die Mitarbeiter an Land und auf See war die Zertifizierung nach ISO 9002. Mit großem Elan haben sie die Vorbereitungsphase der freiwilligen Zertifizierung der Qualitätssicherung bewältigt, ihren Teamgeist intensiviert und sich mit dem Inhaber über die Aushändigung des entsprechenden Zertifikats durch die Klassifikations- und

ing, make excellent use of the outside light. No effort has been spared to provide modern amenities such as air conditioning, ergonomic office furniture and up-to-date communications and data processing equipment.

As shipping company owner, Jürgen Wehr allocates great importance to having well-qualified staff, which recently has increased in response to the expanding fleet. Jürgen Wehr: *"Staff qualifications are a guarantee for performance and reliability in any company, in particular for service providers such as the Oskar Wehr KG (GmbH & Co.). Even the most modern ships at sea and modern offices ashore are useless unless there is reliable, capable personnel to utilize the sophisticated technical equipment on hand. Staff training and re-training is therefore given special emphasis in the company's staffing policy".*
The company prides itself on being able to contribute to the education of young people interested in the shipping profession. Currently, two young women and two young men are presently undergoing training with the company as shipping brokers The shipping training programme comprises business practices, language courses and seminars. At the moment there is also a post open to an economics student for one semester of practical training.

A great challenge for company staff both on shore and on board has been the implementation of ISO 9002 certification. Through concerted action we have managed to master the introductory phase towards voluntary quality management certification while increasing the team spirit within the company. The realization of the certificate by the classification and certification society was enjoyed

Zertifizierungsgesellschaft gefreut. Parallel zur Zertifizierung der Qualitätssicherung an Land wurden auch die Schiffe und ihre Besatzungen für die Erfüllung der ISM-Zertifikate als Teil von SOLAS (Safety of Life at Sea) entsprechend den künftigen Anforderungen in Audits vorbereitet, so daß die Dienstleistungen der Reedereien nun in nahtlosem Zusammenspiel von den Mitarbeitern an Land und auf See höchste Qualität bieten. Der erfolgreiche Abschluß dieser Qualitätssicherung steht als Beispiel dafür, daß die Reederei Wehr stets auf neue Strukturen schnell und umfassend reagiert.

by owner and staff alike. Whilst certification for quality management was being carried out on shore, crews on board were also being trained in preparation for compliance with ISM certificates under the SOLAS regulations (Safety Of Life At Sea) and audits were carried out so that the same high quality of shipping company services could be provided both on land and on board without a hitch. The successful conclusion to the process of quality assurance is another example of how the Wehr shipping company reacts quickly and thoroughly to new structural changes.

Das Büro der Reederei Oskar Wehr in Hamburgs Innenstadt.

The office of Reederei Oskar Wehr in the City of Hamburg.

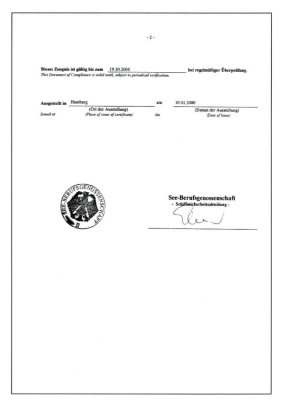

Sprung in die Massengutfahrt und weitere Neubauten

Im Mai 1999 erweiterte die Reederei ihr Betätigungsfeld um einen vierten Flottenbereich nach Kümos, Roll on/Roll off-Schiffen und Containerfrachtern: sie übernahm aus Griechenland vier von einer deutschen Bank finanzierte 65.000-tdw-Bulkcarrier, die alle Anfang Mai 1999 in Hamburg bzw. in Nordeuropa übernommen wurden, weiterhin unter der Flagge Maltas fahren, aber Namen aus der Sylter Familie Selmer erhielten, aus der Helga Wehr, Gattin des Firmengründers, stammt:
HUGO SELMER ex TOMIS HOPE
THOMAS SELMER ex TOMIS GLORY
FREDERIKE SELMER ex TOMIS SPIRIT
MIMI SELMER ex TOMIS FAITH
Das 1985/7 im rumänischen Mangalia entstandene Bulker-Quartett wurde nach der Übernahme sukzessive auf neuen technischen Wartungs- und Ausrüstungsstand gebracht und von der eigenen Befrachtung auf dem Spotmarkt beschäftigt.

Additional bulk trade, more new shipbuilding

In May 1999 the company extended its three basic spheres of activities – short sea shipping, roll on-roll off and container transport – to include a fourth: bulk carriers. Wehr acquired four Greek-owned 65,000-tdw bulk carriers which were financed by a German bank. Delivery of all four was taken in early May 1999 by their new owners in Hamburg The vessels will continue to trade under Maltese flag but their names were changed to honour the Selmer family in Sylt, where Helga Wehr (née Selmer) was born. They are:
the HUGO SELMER, the ex-TOMIS HOPE
the THOMAS SELMER, the ex-TOMIS GLORY
the FREDERIKE SELMER, the ex-TOMIS SPIRIT and
the MIMI SELMER, the ex-TOMIS FAITH.
The four bulk carriers were built in Rumania (Mangalia) in 1985/87 and following delivery they were successively upgraded to high levels of maintenance and equipment standards. The company carries out its own freight

Massengutfrachter MIMI SELMER kurz nach der Übernahme in Hamburg.

Bulkcarrier MIMI SELMER shortly after take-over at Hamburg.

Massengutfrachter THOMAS SELMER auslaufend Antwerpen mit Getreide für den Iran.

Bulkcarrier THOMAS SELMER leaving Antwerp with grain for Iran.

Knapp ein Jahr später vergrößerte die Reederei ihre Flotte erneut. 'Die Einführung des Tonnagesteuersystems hat uns veranlaßt, unseren Schiffspark in Deutschland auszubauen und die Bereederungsaktivitäten unserer Unternehmensgruppe in Hamburg zu verstärken. Dies sichert die Beschäftigung unseres Mitarbeiterstabes an Land wie an Bord', erklärte Jürgen Wehr anläßlich des Ankaufs zweier weiterer Containerschiffe durch das Unternehmen am 19. April 2000 in Hamburg. Angekauft wurden zwei noch fast werftneue Schiffe des bewährten Typs 'B 170', die im November bzw. Dezember 1999 von der polnischen Werft Stocznia Szczecinska Porta Holding SA an die chilenische Compania Sud Americana de Vapores SA als ELQUI und ILLAPEL übergeben worden waren. Die Übernahme der ILLAPEL (Reedereiname WEHR BLANKENESE) erfolgte am 27. April 2000 in San Antonio / Chile, die der ELQUI (WEHR SCHULAU) Mitte Mai in Brasilien.

Mit diesen Ankäufen hatte die Reederei ihre Flotte seit 1996 um 13 Einheiten ausgebaut,

brokerage for the ships, which are currently trading on the spot market.
Less than a year later the fleet was once again enlarged. Jürgen Wehr explained why on 19th April 2000 in Hamburg, when the company purchased two more container ships. *"The introduction of tonnage tax has moved us to increase our fleet in Germany and strengthen group shipping activities in Hamburg. This should guarantee jobs both ashore and afloat."* The ships he referred to were two nearly-new vessels – again of the B 170 type, which had already proved its worth. In November and December 1999 they were delivered as the ELQUI and the ILLAPEL to their Chilean owners, Compañia Sud Americana de Vapores SA, by the Polish shipyard Stocznia Szczecinska Porta Holding SA. Wehr took delivery of the ILLAPEL (renamed WEHR BLANKENESE) on the 27th April 2000 in San Antonio/Chile, and of the ELQUI (renamed WEHR SCHULAU) in mid-May in Brazil.
Since 1996 Wehr has expanded its fleet by thirteen vessels, including the two latest ships: nine newly-built container ships and four

nämlich um neun Containerschiffsneubauten und vier Panmax-Bulker. Acht der Containerschiffe sind Schwestern und gehören dem Typ B 170 an, die ILLAPEL lief im übrigen als 100. Containerfrachter der Stocznia Szczecinska vom Stapel. Begonnen hatten die Polen ihre Erfolgsserie am 20. Dezember 1991 mit der Ablieferung der KAIRO (1012 TEU) vom Typ B 183, der wiederum auf dem bewährten Typ RW 39 der Bremerhavener Rickmers-Werft basiert. Im Mai 2000 bestellte die Reederei Oskar Wehr bei Stocznia Szczecinska nochmals zwei Neubauten des Typs B 170 mit 1730 TEU, deren Auslieferung für das vierte Quartal 2001 vereinbart wurde. Sie wird dann zehn Einheiten dieses Typs disponieren.

Ebenfalls im vierten Quartal 2001 sollen zwei 33.600 tdw-Containerschiffe für 2524 TEU und 21,5 Knoten Geschwindigkeit abgeliefert werden, für die Jürgen Wehr im Juni 2000 die Bauverträge mit der Kvaerner Warnow Werft in Warnemünde unterschrieb. Wenig später übernahm die Reederei die Bauverträge für zwei gleich große Containerschiffe des Typs VW 2500.1 bei der Volkswerft in Stralsund, die im Mai und Juli 2002 in Fahrt kommen sollen. Im Dezember 2000 erweiterte die Reederei den Auftrag bei Kvaerner Warnow um zwei weitere auf vier 2524 TEU-Schiffe, die im Anschluß an die bereits bestellten geliefert werden. Mit diesen sechs 2524 TEU-Containerschiffen wird die Reederei dann auch in einem weiteren Segment des Containerschiffsmarktes tätig sein. Die Flotte wird dann 24 Schiffe umfassen; sicherlich nicht der Schlußpunkt einer expansiven, aber soliden Familienreederei.

Panmax bulk carriers. Of the container ships, eight are sister ships of the B 170 type. The ILLAPEL also happened to be the 100th containership to be launched by Stocznia Szczecinska. The Polish shipyard commenced the successful series on 20th December 1991, when delivery was taken of the KAIRO (1,012 TEU). The ship was a B 183-type vessel, which in its turn was based on the former RW 39 type from the Rickmers yard in Bremerhaven and had many times proved its worth. In May 2000 the Oskar Wehr shipping company again ordered two more B 170-type container ships of 1,730 TEU each from Stocznia Szczecinska, for delivery in the fourth quarter of 2001. This will bring the number of units of this type operated by Wehr up to ten.

Also to be delivered in the fourth quarter of 2001 are two containerships of 33,600 tdw and 2,524 TEU capacity and a speed of 21.5 knots. Jürgen Wehr contracted the new CV 2500-type ships from the Kvaerner Warnow shipyard in Warnemünde in June 2000. Shortly thereafter Oskar Wehr shipping company assumed the contracts for two container ships of similar size with the Volkswerft Stralsund (of the VW 2500.1 type). In December 2000 the company increased its orders at the Kvaerner Warnow yard from two to a total of four ships of 2,524 TEU, the additional ships to be delivered after the first order had been supplied. The vessels will lead Wehr into yet another sphere of the container shipping market, bringing the fleet up to a total of 24 ships. With such a rich history and sound basis, these ships will certainly not be the last for the family-owned shipping company.

Der Reeder und seine langjährigen Mitarbeiter

Reeder Jürgen Wehr kann bei der Führung seines mittelständischen Schiffahrtsbetriebes auf z. T. langjährig bewährte Mitarbeiter in allen Abteilungen vertrauen. In der Leitung wird er von Prokuristen bzw. in der Maklerfirma Wehr Transport von einem Geschäftsführer unterstützt.

Reinhold Meyer, Jahrgang 1949, ist Prokurist und Leiter der Buchhaltung. Bis 1977 ließ die damals noch wesentlich kleinere Reederei Oskar Wehr ihre Buchhaltung von einem Steuerberater außer Haus machen. 1977 machte die gewachsene Flotte die Schaffung einer eigenen Buchhaltung erforderlich. Oskar Wehr, allen Innovationen gegenüber aufgeschlossen, ließ sich von seinem Sohn Jürgen zum Kauf einer EDV-Anlage überzeugen. Der Kienzle-Rechner, der ein ganzes Zimmer füllte und mit immer gleichbleibender Temperatur bei Laune gehalten werden mußte, war der erste dieser Größenordnung in einer Hamburger Reederei. Mit dem Rechner kam Reinhold Meyer, der die Reederei nicht nur durch alle folgenden technischen Entwicklungen der Rechnergenerationen führte, sondern auch die Reederei sicher in allen Buchhaltungs- und Finanzfragen vertrat. Seit vielen Jahren leitet er als Prokurist diese Abteilung und ist Mitglied der Geschäftsführung.

Ebenfalls 1977 kam der Schiffsingenieur Dieter Grundmann (Jahrgang 1946) zur Reederei. Er fuhr zunächst als leitender Ingenieur bei

The ship owner, the shipping company

The shipping company is a small to medium-sized business. As ship owner, Jürgen Wehr is backed by an experienced staff with many years of experience in all departments. This includes the Managing Director for the company's shipping brokers, Wehr Transport.

Reinhold Meyer was born in 1949 and is chief executive in the company, member of the Board of Directors while heading the Accounting Department. Accounts for the Oskar Wehr shipping company were traditionally handled by an outside tax accountant until 1977, when the growing fleet forced the company to open its own accounting department. In compliance to his reputation of liberal open-mindedness, Oskar Wehr was persuaded by his son to invest in computers. The Kienzle computer which was purchased filled a whole room and had to be kept at a constant temperature to keep it running. It was the first large-capacity computer to be employed at a Hamburg shipping company. Reinhold Meyer started work at the company with the computer. He has not only steered the company through all the technical innovations but also remained a confident representative of the company in all accounting and financial matters.

In the same year (1977) Dieter Grundmann also joined the company. He was born in 1946 and had a ship's engineer's training. After a career at sea as Chief Engineer with Wehr, he joined the shore-based staff on 15th

Wehr zur See, und ist seit dem 15. November 1979 an Land, als er nämlich zum Inspektor berufen wurde. Seither beaufsichtigt er die turnusmäßige Wartung der Flotte, hat ungezählte Problemchen und Probleme gelöst und alle Neubauten von der Planung bis zur Ablieferung begleitet. In den vielen Jahren seiner Inspektionstätigkeit sammelte Dieter Grundmann umfangreiche Erfahrungen, die er nachwachsenden Inspektoren weitergibt, wie ihm die Förderung des Nachwuchses allgemein ein besonderes Anliegen ist. Mit seinem Erfahrungsschatz hilft er auch Kapitänen, den Leitenden Ingenieuren und Offizieren, die Probleme des täglichen Schiffsbetriebs leichter zu meistern. Als Prokurist ist er für die gesamte Flotte, die Inspektion, Einkauf und seefahrendes Personal zuständig. Er ist Mitglied der Geschäftsführung.

Den Schiffahrtskaufmann Eckehard Nemitz (Jahrgang 1957) kennt Reeder Jürgen Wehr schon seit seiner frühesten Befrachtungstätigkeit nach Beendigung der Ausbildung. 1983 begann er seine Tätigkeit als Befrachter in der damaligen 'one man show' Wehr Transport. Er verlagerte die Tätigkeitsbereiche so schnell und erfolgreich von der Küstenschiffahrt in die Große Fahrt, daß er bald zum Geschäftsführer berufen wurde. In dieser Position ist er heute noch aktiv. Er befrachtet mit seinem Team die Wehr-Flotte und betreibt darüber hinaus ein aktives Fremdbefrachtungsgeschäft. Eckehard Nemitz zählt heute zu den namhaften Containerschiffsmaklern im internationalen Geschäft.

Jürgen Wehr: 'Ich bin stolz auf diese und meine anderen Mitarbeiter und Mitarbeiterin-

November 1979, when he was appointed Engineering Superintendent. Since then his job has been to supervise routine maintenance for the Wehr fleet. His capabilities include solving problems of all kinds, large and small, and overseeing all newbuilding projects from drawing-board to final delivery. All the experience Dieter Grundmann has gained over the years as Engineering Superintendent has been passed on to the next generation superintendents. In fact giving support to the younger generation is one of his special interests. His wealth of experience is also an assistance to masters, chief engineers and officers alike when coping with day-to-day running problems on a ship. As a chief executive, Dieter Grundmann is responsible for the whole fleet and for the Engineering Supervision, Purchasing and Seagoing Personnel departments. He too is a member of the Board of Directors.

Eckehard Nemitz was born in 1957 and trained as a shipping clerk. He first met Jürgen Wehr, the owner of the company, after completing his training as an apprenticeship clerk. In 1983 he started working on his own as freighting expert for Wehr Transport. He expanded his activities from coastal to ocean-going shipping with such speed and expertise that he was soon made Managing Director. This is a post he still holds. Together with his team he is responsible for making chartering arrangements for the Wehr fleet which also includes competitive chartering. Eckehard Nemitz has made a name for himself internationally as a specialist broker for container shipping.

To quote Jürgen Wehr: "I am proud of my directors – indeed of all my staff. Without their

nen, ohne die die erfolgsorientierte und auch in Krisenzeiten sichere Führung der Reederei so nicht möglich gewesen wäre; ihnen, und allen Kapitänen und Besatzungsmitgliedern gilt an dieser Stelle mein Dank.'

motivation it would not have been possible to steer the company on such a straight course through the good times and the bad. May I take this opportunity to thank them all – both ashore and at sea."

Reeder Jürgen Wehr (Mitte) kann nicht nur auf langjährige Mitarbeiter vertrauen, auch Arnold Fölsch (links) und Werner Schultz, schon Partner seines Vaters, halten ihm die Treue.

Not only can ship owner Jürgen Wehr (centre) rely on a team of many years; Arnold Fölsch (left) and Werner Schultz (right), both partners of his late father, also remain faithful to him and to his company.

Die Flotte / The Fleet

ANNE – 80 GRT – 1945-1954

HELGA WEHR (1) – 350 GRT – 1919/1954-1967

JÜRGEN WEHR (1) – 424 GRT – 1957-1960

JÜRGEN WEHR (1) after lengthening – 498 GRT – 1960-1971

MARIANNE WEHR – 499 GRT – 1957/1963-1963

GABRIELE WEHR (1) – 499 GRT – 1965-1978

HELGA WEHR (2) – 1190 GRT – 1966-1982

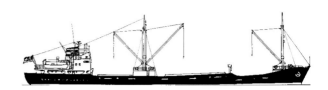

HUGO SELMER (1) – 1471 GRT – 1956/1968-1973

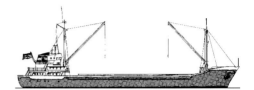

JANNE WEHR (1) – 420 GRT – 1968-1974

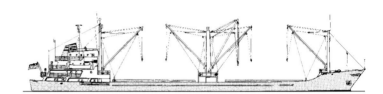

HARTFORD EXPRESS – 3259 GRT – 1970-1982

JÜRGEN WEHR (2) – 499 GRT – 1973-1981

JÜRGEN WEHR (2) after lengthening – 874 GRT – 1981-1993

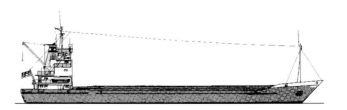

JANNE WEHR (2) – 999 GRT – 1974-1981

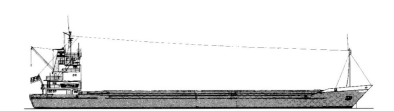
*JANNE WEHR (2) after lengthening –
1599 GRT – 1981-*

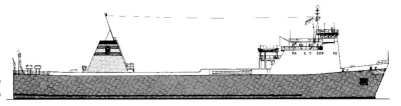
*THOMAS WEHR
GABRIELE WEHR (2) – 1599 GRT
1977-1982
1978-1982*

*THOMAS WEHR
GABRIELE WEHR (2)
after lengthening –
2185 GRT – 1982-
1982-*

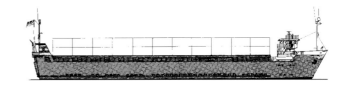
SIGRID WEHR (1) – 999 GRT – 1978-1981

*SIGRID WEHR after lengthening –
1600 GRT – 1981-1989*

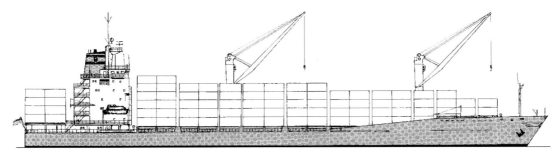
HELGA WEHR (3) – 13,476 GRT – 1983-2000

CAROLINE – 1599 GRT – 1978/1989-1993
CHRISTINE – 1599 GRT – 1977/1989-1993
SIGRID – 1599 GRT – 1977/1989-1993

BIRTE WEHR – 999 GRT – 1982/1990-1999

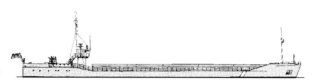

IMKE WEHR –
6819 GRT – 1985/1992-1999

PETER WEHR (2) –
6819 GRT – 1986/-1992-1996

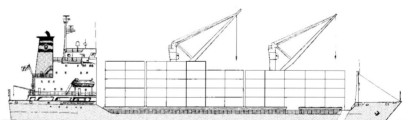

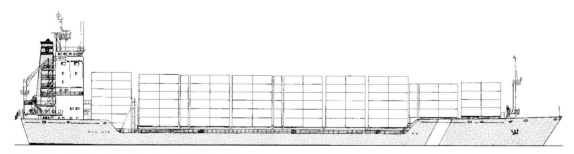

WEHR Newbuilding No. 293 – 15,500 GRT – sold during construction
WEHR Newbuilding No. 294 – 15,500 GRT – sold during construction

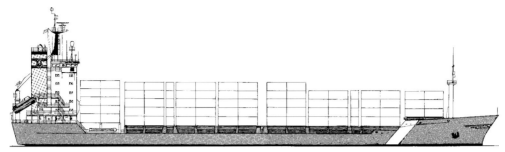

SIGRID WEHR (2) – 10,917 GT – 1995-

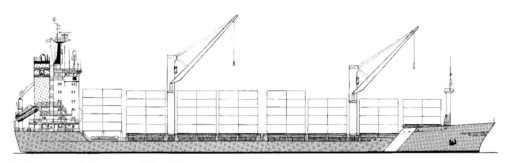

SIGRID WEHR (2) – 10,917 GT – 1995-
SIGRID WEHR (2) with cranes since 1997

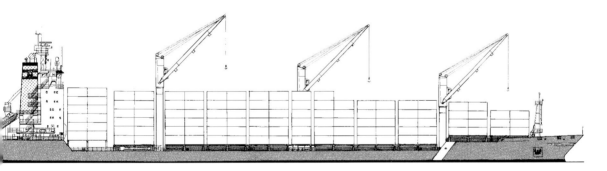

WEHR ALTONA – 16,801 GT – 1997-
WEHR OTTENSEN – 16,801 GT – 1997-
WEHR KOBLENZ – 16,801 GT – 1998-
WEHR MÜDEN – 16,801 GT – 1998-
WEHR FLOTTBEK – 16,801 GT – 1999-
WEHR RISSEN – 16,801 GT – 1999-
WEHR BLANKENESE – 16,801 GT – 1999-
WEHR SCHULAU – 16,801 GT – 1999-
WEHR NIENSTEDTEN – 16,801 GT – 2001-
WEHR FALKENSTEIN – 16,801 GT – 2001-

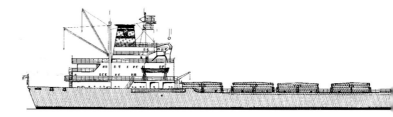

HUGO SELMER (2) – 39,537 GT – 1999-
MIMI SELMER – 39,537 GT – 1999-
THOMAS SELMER – 39,537 GT – 1999-
FREDERIKE SELMER – 39,537 GT – 1999-

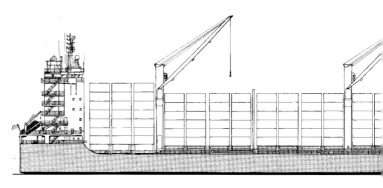

WEHR ELBE – 2524 TEU – 2001-
WEHR WESER – 2524 TEU – 2001-
WEHR TRAVE – 2524 TEU – 2002-
WEHR WARNOW – 2524 TEU – 2002-
WEHR TBN 1 – 2524 TEU – 2002-
WEHR TBN 2 – 2524 TEU – 2002-

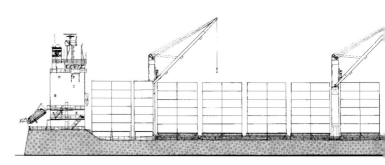

WEHR ALSTER – 2524 TEU – 2002-
WEHR BILLE – 2524 TEU – 2002-

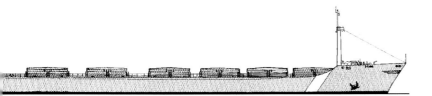

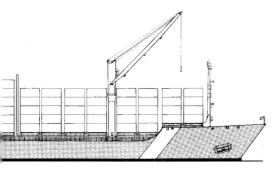

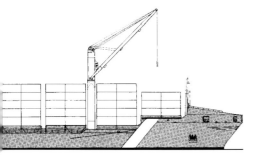

List of Ships

1) ANNE in Warwisch.

1) 2-masted ever ANNE

DEAT – 80 GRT – 24.74 x 4.94 x 2.00 m – 1 four-stroke three-cylinder Jastram engine, 90 HPe

1906 completed by J. Sietas, Cranz, as ANNE for Carsten Raap, Krautsand (DEU). 1945 sunk in Hamburg by aircraft bombs. July 1945 sold in submerged condition to Oskar Wehr, Hamburg (DEU). 1945/47 repaired at Wolkau-Werft, Wilhelmsburg. 1947 back in service. March 1952 lengthened at Grube-Werft, Warwisch/Elbe, by six metres, now 98 GRT/160 tdw. 1954 sold to Wilhelm Siems, Bützfleth. In April 1962 sold to Martin Rohden, Ilowerfehn, port of registry Oldersum. 1.2.1965 handed over to Rolf Rohden, Oldersum. 1970 deleted from Register.

2) Singledeck motorship HELGA WEHR (1)

DAGZ – 350 GRT / 539 tdw – 47.30 x 7.70 x 4.20 m – 1 four-stroke six-cylinder MaK engine, 300 HPe

8.10.1919 launched. 1919 completed by Joh. C. Tecklenborg AG, Geestemünde, as steam trawler LUDWIG SANDERS (249 GRT, 38.80 x 7.17 x 2.97 m, one triple-expansion engine, 420 HP, made by the builders, call sign KRQL/DEXY) for Carl Kämpf, Geestemünde (DEU). 1924 registered at Wesermünde-G. (DEU). August 1928 sold to Kämpf & Meyer. August 1929 sold to Hochseefischerei Kämpf Partenreederei. August 1940 transferred to Kriegsmarine, intended for 'Seelöwe' operation. December 1940 redelivered to owners. 19.1.1952 sold to H. Peill, Stade (DEU), renamed DÖRTE. Converted until April 1953 by Gebr. Wandmaker & Co., Wilhelmsburg, into a motor coaster with data as mentioned above. 9.6.1954 sold to Oskar Wehr, Hamburg (DEU). 23.7.1957 renamed HELGA WEHR. 12.1.1966 renamed ILSE H. 20.6.1967 sold to Fritz Heidemann, Hamburg (DEU). 2.4.1969 on voyage from Maassluis to Runcorn with cargo of chemicals in position 51.49,51 N 03.54,8 E off Hoek van Holland vessel capsized and sank when heavy deckcargo shifted. June/July 1969 salvaged in two parts which were beached at the entrance of Nieuwe Waterweg and broken up there.

2) DÖRTE wurde HELGA WEHR (1)
2) DÖRTE became the HELGA WEHR (1)

3) Singledeck motorship
JÜRGEN WEHR (1)

DGXU – 424 GRT / 700 tdw – 47.62 x 8.94 x 3.80 m – 1 four-stroke six-cylinder Klöckner-Humboldt-Deutz engine, 300 HPe

12.10.1957 launched. 14.11.1957 completed by J. J. Sietas Schiffswerft, Neuenfelde (No. 426) as JÜRGEN WEHR for Oskar Wehr, Hamburg (DEU). September 1960 lengthened by her builders, now 498 GRT/834 tdw, 55.32 x 8.94 x 3.80 m. 12.2.1971 sold to Wolfgang Wulff, Hamburg (DEU), Transmar Schiffahrtskontor Adolf Feindt appointed as managing owners. 23.2. 1971 renamed DUVENSTEDT. 9.5.1973 until 22.10.1976 registered at Mogadiscio (SOM). 13.10.1976 sold to MS. 'Santa Angelika' KG Marienthaler Vermögensgesellschaft mbH & Co., Hamburg. 23.10.1976 registered at Panama (PAN). 12.11.1976 renamed SANTA ANGELIKA. 6.7.1977 sold to Andromache de Panama Shipping Co SA, Panama, renamed ANDROMACHE I. 11.3.1984 sank off the Libyan coast in a storm.

3) JÜRGEN WEHR (1)

4) Singledeck motorship
MARIANNE WEHR

DIPJ – 499 GRT / 937 tdw – 58.04 x 9.64 x 3.96 m – 1 four-stroke eight-cylinder MaK engine with 675 HPe

31.1.1957 launched. 30.3.1957 completed by Hugo Peters, Wewelsfleth (No. 485-82) as HOHENBUCHEN for Partenreederei, Hamburg (DEU), Poseidon Schiffahrts GmbH appointed as managing owners. 1.2.1963 sold to Oskar Wehr, Hamburg, renamed MARIANNE WEHR. 14.10.1963 sank near ELBE I lightvessel in position 54.00 N 08.11 E in heavy weather when freak wave pooped the ship. Her crew of nine was lost.

4) MARIANNE WEHR

5) Tweendeck motorship
GABRIELE WEHR (1) / GABRIELE W

DNIE – 499 GRT / 1182 tdw – 62.66 x 10.52 x 6.55 m – 1 four-stroke 6-cylinder Klöckner-Humboldt-Deutz engine, 900 HPe

19.12.1965 launched. 31.12.1965 completed by J. J. Sietas Schiffswerft, Neuenfelde (No. 555) as GABRIELE WEHR for Oskar Wehr, Hamburg (DEU). 1974 transferred to Oskar Wehr KG. 9.3.1978 renamed GABRIELE W – 31.10.1978 sold to Heinz Suhr, Hamburg, renamed HEINZ SUHR. 12.8.1986 until 1.8.1988 registered in San Lorenzo (HND). 1.8.1988 until 17.1.1989 registered Kingstown (VCT). 17.1.1990 registered in St. John's (ATG). 8.6.1995 abandoned by crew in a storm off the Netherlands coast when on a voyage from Lettland to Great Britain with timber. Sank 9.6.1995.

5) GABRIELE WEHR (1)

7) HUGO SELMER

6) **Tweendeck motorship**
   HELGA WEHR (2)
DHHW – 499 / 1190 GRT – 1245 / 2123 tdw – 71.33 x 10.82 x 6.55 m – 1 four-stroke eight-cylinder Klöckner-Humboldt-Deutz engine, 1320 HPe

5.2.1966 launched. 8.3.1966 completed by J. J. Sietas Schiffswerft, Neuenfelde (No. 573) as HELGA WEHR for Oskar Wehr, Hamburg (DEU). 1982 transferred to Oskar Wehr KG. 10.1982 sold to Karl Heinz Eimann, Hamburg, renamed STEFAN E. 11.6.1982 registered at Panama (PAN). 23.3.1987 whilst on voyage from Antwerp to Monrovia north of Dakar sank in position 17.04 N / 18.04 W. Seven survivors and one body were rescued.

7) **Singledeck motorship**
   HUGO SELMER (1)
DHHS – 1471 GRT / 2713 tdw – 74.82 x 11.71 x 5.11 m – four-stroke six-cylinder Klöckner-Humboldt-Deutz engine, 1250 HPe

24.1.1956 launched. 10.4.1956 completed by Jos. L. Meyer, Papenburg (No. 472) as FLEETWING for Granta Steamship Co. Ltd., Newcastle (GBR), Witherington & Everett appointed as managing owners. 1959 sold to Pargas Kalkberg AB, Åbo (FIN), OY Semtrans appointed as managing owners, renamed FALLSUND. 20.5.1968 sold to Partenreederei, Hamburg (DEU), Oskar Wehr appointed as managing owner, renamed HUGO SELMER. July 1968 reconditioned by her builders. 7.6.1973 sold to A. Tricoli, Napoli (ITA), renamed ADELINA TRICOLI. 1982 sold to A. Merzario, Napoli. 1982 sold to Eurofer SpA, Napoli. 24.11.1982 handed over to A. Merzario for demolition at San Giorgio di Nogaro, which commenced 29.12.1982 at Cantieri Nav. Santa Marta.

6) HELGA WEHR (2)

8) JANNE WEHR (1)

8) Semi containership
JANNE WEHR (1)

DHJW – *420 GRT / 1112 tdw / 63 TEU – 65.31 x 11.03 x 6.05 m – 1 four-stroke six-cylinder MWM engine, 500 HPe*

6.9.1968 launched. 18.10.1968 completed by Scheepswerf Hoogezand NV, Bergum (No. 145) as JANNE WEHR for Oskar Wehr, Hamburg (DEU). 1972 converted to an open/closed shelterdecker, now also 992 GRT/2012 tdw. 4.1.1974 sold to G. Hadjigiannis, Piraeus (GRC), renamed BILLY. 1974 sold to Santamar Maritime Co. Ltd., Famagusta (CYP). 1975 registered at Limassol (CYP). 1979 sold to Mina Line S. A. L., Tripoli (LBN), renamed MINA I. 1979 sold to H. A. Sattout & Co., Tripoli. 1984 to E. N. Moubayed & Co, Tripoli. 1984 renamed CAROL S. 1986 sold to Virginia Express Navigation Co. Ltd., San Lorenzo (HND), Seadoll Chartering Co. Ltd. appointed as managing owners, renamed VIRGINIA. 1988 sold to Unity Navigation Cia S. de RL, San Lorenzo, renamed UNITY I. 1994 sold to Continental Maritime Co. SA., San Lorenzo. 1997 newly measured, now 1153 GT/2025 tdw. 1999 sold to unnamed buyers at San Lorenzo, renamed VIGLA. 2001 still trading.

9) Semi containership
HARTFORD EXPRESS /
CONTI HOLANDIA

DAPW – *1558 / 3259 GRT – 3145/5085 tdw – 184 TEU – 99.82 x 15.44 x 6.22 m – one four-stroke eight-cylinder Klöckner-Humboldt-Deutz engine, 3000 HPe*

21.8.1970 launched as PETER WEHR. 29.9.1970 completed by Jos. L. Meyer, Papenburg (No. 557) as HARTFORD EXPRESS for Partenreederei, Hamburg (DEU), Oskar Wehr appointed as managing owner. 1976 owners style changed to

9) HARTFORD EXPRESS

Oskar Wehr KG. 4.11.1981 renamed CONTI HOLANDIA. 19.5.1982 renamed HARTFORD EXPRESS. 4.11.1982 sold to Read Sea Maritime Services, Panama (PAN), renamed BLUE MARLIN. 1983 sold to Government of the Peoples Republic of China (CHN), renamed QU JIANG. 1986 sold to Zhejiang Ocean Shipping Co., COSCO Zhejiang appointed as managing owners. 2001 still trading.

10) Tweendeck motorship
JÜRGEN WEHR (2) / JÜRGEN W

DNJW – *499 GRT / 1585 tdw – 72.22 x 11.83 x 3.88 m – one four-stroke 12-cylinder Klöckner-Humboldt-Deutz engine, 1085 kW*

10.10.1973 completed by J. J. Sietas Schiffswerft, Neuenfelde (No. 701) as JÜRGEN WEHR for Oskar Wehr, Hamburg (DEU). 1976 transferred to Oskar Wehr KG. 26.7.1977 renamed JÜRGEN W. 15.3.1978 renamed JÜRGEN WEHR. November 1981 lengthened by Szcecinska Stocznia Remontawa, Szczecin, now 874 GRT / 2435 tdw, 82.74 x 11.80 x 6.6 m. 1985 installation of a new MaK engine with 1000 kW. 28.6.1989 sold to Jürgen Wehr, Hamburg, Os-

10) JÜRGEN WEHR (1)

kar Wehr KG (GmbH & Co.) appointed as managing owners. 11.4.1991 flagged out to Antigua and Barbuda. 15.7.1993 sold to Tarco Nord AS, Nyborg (DNK), renamed JÜRGEN. 18.8.1983 called at Swinoujscie to be converted to an asphalt tanker. 8.11.1993 sold to Four Partners Shipping AS, Kristiansand (NIS). In January 1994 renamed VISCARIA, newly measured, now 1859 GT/2084 tdw. 1996 mgrs. Elat Shipping AS and in 1997 sold to them, mgrs. A. K. Aagesen & Partners AS. 2001 still trading.

11) JANNE WEHR (2)

11) **Containership JANNE WEHR (2) / ROXANE KERSTEN / CONTAINERSHIPS I / THAMES STAR**

DGFW – *999 GRT / 2600 tdw / 185 TEU – 89.76 x 14.53 x 4.86 m – 1 four-stroke eight-cylinder Klöckner-Humboldt-Deutz engine, 2206 kW*

8.5.1974 launched. 14.6.1974 completed by J. J. Sietas Schiffswerft, Neuenfelde (No. 742) as JANNE WEHR for Oskar Wehr, Hamburg (DEU). 3.6.1960 renamed ROXANE KERSTEN. 29.6.1981 renamed JANNE WEHR. July 1981 lengthened by Szczecinska Stocznia Remontawa, Szczecin, now 1599 GRT/4020 tdw / 256 TEU, 106.57 x 14.50 x 7.56 m. 9.9.1981 renamed ROXANE KERSTEN. 10.5.1983 renamed JANNE WEHR. 15.1.1985 renamed CONTAINERSHIPS I. 13.4.1987 re-named JANNE WEHR. 28.6.1989 sold to Jürgen Wehr, Hamburg, Oskar Wehr KG (GmbH & Co), appointed as managing owners. 13.7.1992 sold to S & C Wehr Transport GmbH & Co. KG, Oskar Wehr KG (GmbH & Co.) appointed as managing owners. 8.9.1992 flagged out to Antigua and Barbuda (ATG). 11.3.1994 reflagged to Germany (DEU). 1994 newly measured and converted in Poland into a boxshaped vessel, now 3287 GT/4020 tdw, 97.91 x 14.50 x 7.95/4.58 m. 1995 registered at Funafuti (TUV) and re-named THAMES STAR. 1997 transferred to Partenreederei, mgrs. as before. Sold in 2001, still trading.

12) **Roll on/Roll off motorship WACRO EXPRESS / THOMAS WEHR / TOR NEERLANDIA / DANA GERMANIA / MANA / SANTA MARIA / FULDATAL / HORNLINK**

DHNW – *1599 GRT / 2900 tdw / 71 trailers / 140 TEU plus 37 cars – 108.30 x 17.42 x 5.26 m – 2 four-stroke eight-cylinder MaK engines, 2207 kW each*

12) THOMAS WEHR

18.1.1977 launched as THOMAS WEHR. 22.4. 1977 completed by Rickmers Rhederei GmbH Rickmers Werft, Bremerhaven as WACRO EXPRESS for Partenreederei, Hamburg (DEU), Oskar Wehr KG appointed as managing owners. 17.4.1978 renamed THOMAS WEHR. August 1982 lengthened by Werft Nobiskrug GmbH by 25 metres, now 2185 GRT/4190 tdw, 271 TEU / 91 trailers, 141.30 x 17.40 x 5.70 m. 23.8.1982 renamed TOR NEERLANDIA. 21.6.1985 renamed DANA GERMANIA. 17.12.1986 renamed THOMAS WEHR. 1.2.1992 renamed MANA and flagged out to Antigua and Barbuda (ATG). 31.3.1993 renamed SANTA MARIA. 4.10.1993 renamed FULDATAL. Februray 1994 renamed HORNLINK. 1995 renamed THOMAS WEHR and newly measured, now 7628 GT/4322 tdw. 1998 registered at Funafuti (TUV). 2001 still trading.

13) Roll on/Roll off motorship GABRIELE WEHR (2) / TOR ANGLIA / SARI

DNGW – *1599 GRT / 2866 tdw / 140 TEU / 71 trailers plus 37 cars – 108.31 x 17.42 x 5.26 m – 2 four-stroke eight-cylinder MaK engines, 2207 kW each*

14.3.1978 launched. 8.6.1978 completed by Rickmers Rhederei GmbH, Rickmers Werft, Bremerhaven (No. 391) as GABRIELE WEHR for Partenreederei, Hamburg (DEU), Oskar Wehr KG appointed as managing owners. July 1982 lengthened by Werft Nobiskrug GmbH, Rendsburg, by 25 metres, now 2185 GRT / 4322 tdw, 271 TEU / 91 trailers, 141.30 x 17.40 x 5.70 m. 2.8.1982 renamed TOR ANGLIA. 8.7.1985 renamed GABRIELE WEHR. 21.12.1992 renamed SARI and transferred to Antigua and Barbuda flag (ATG). 27.4.1993 renamed GA-

13) GABRIELE WEHR (2)

BRIELE WEHR. 1994 newly measured, now 7635 GT/4322 tdw. 18.12.1994 registered at Funafuti (TUV). 1995 reflagged to Germany and registered in Hamburg. 2001 still trading.

14) Roll on / Roll off motorship SIGRID WEHR

DGPS – *999 GRT / 3000 tdw / 294 TEU / 36 trailers – 84.25 x 18.02 x 3.63 m – 2 four-stroke eight-cylinder MaK engines, 1200 kW each*

25.1.1978 launched at Stahlbauabteilung of Howaldtswerke/Deutsche Werft AG, Kiel-Dietrichsdorf. Thereafter towed to Kremer Werft GmbH (Ulrich Harms) (No. 1188), Glückstadt, for fitting out. After Kremer went into bankruptcy 1978 towed to Rickmers Rhederei GmbH, Rickmers Werft, Bremerhaven for completion. 9.9.1978 completed as SIGRID WEHR for

14) SIGRID WEHR

Partenreederei, Hamburg (DEU), Oskar Wehr KG appointed as managing owners. September 1981 lengthened by Stocznia Szczecinska Remontowa, Szczecin, now 1600 GRT/4519 tdw / 35 trailers / 336 TEU, 110.77 x 18.00 x 9.20 m. 8.6.1989 sold to A. Gerrards Rederi, Bergen (NOR), renamed GERORO. 1991 sold to Skua Shipping Co. Ltd., Kingstown (VCT), renamed FAIRLIGHT. 1992 sold to Iran Marine Services Co., Bandar Abbas (IRN), renamed PISHRO. 2001 still trading.

15) **Container motorship
HELGA WEHR (3) / NORASIA HELGA / MAERSK CLAUDINE / MAERSK BELLA / ASIAN SENATOR / HARTFORD EXPRESS (2) / CMB ENERGY / KADUNA / CITY OF AMSTERDAM / SPIRIT OF AMSTERDAM / P & O NEDLLOYD CARACAS**
DHWK – *13,476 GT / 19,440 tdw / 1152 TEU – 152.80 x 23.00 x 13.70 m – 1 four-stroke eight-cylinder MaK engine, 6899 kW*
24.11.1973 completed AG Weser Seebeckwerft, Bremerhaven (No. 1044) as HELGA WEHR for Oskar Wehr Schiffahrt & Beteiligungs KG, Hamburg (DEU), Oskar Wehr KG appointed as managing owners. 2.3.1984 renamed NORASIA HELGA. 13.12.1984 renamed HELGA WEHR. 8.7.1985 renamed MAERSK CLAUDINE. 20.12.1985 renamed HELGA WEHR. 26.3.1986 renamed MAERSK BELLA. 7.4.1987 renamed HELGA WEHR. 27.4.1987 renamed ASIAN SENATOR. 19.10.1987 renamed HELGA WEHR. 3.11.1988 renamed HARTFORD EXPRESS (2). 10.7.1989 renamed CMB ENERGY. 23.10.1990 renamed HELGA WEHR. 5.7.1991 renamed KADUNA. 12.2.1992 renamed CITY OF AMSTERDAM. 27.3.1993 renamed SPIRIT OF AMSTERDAM. 9.6.1993 renamed HELGA WEHR. 14.9.1993 renamed CMB ENERGY. 1995 flagged out to Liberia, registered at Monrovia (LBR). 1997 renamed P & O NEDLLOYD CARACAS. 1998 renamed HELGA WEHR. 2000 sold to Adria Maritime SpA, Trieste (ITA) and handed over in Antwerp 6.12.2000, renamed ADRIA BIANCA. 2001 still trading.

16) FJORD STAR ex CAROLINE

16) **Singledeck motorship CAROLINE
VSQD –** *1599 GRT / 3050 tdw – 80.68 x 14.33 x 5.11 m – 1 four-stroke six-cylinder MWM engine, 2205 kW*
26.1.1978 launched. March 1978 completed by Scheepswerf 'Waterhuizen' NV J. Pattje, Waterhuizen (No. 335) as ALTAPPEN for BV Equator, Delfzijl (NLD). 1983 Befrachtungskontor Schöning GmbH, Haren, appointed as managing owners. 1986 sold to Noordlijn Holding BV, Delfzijl, NORA Reederei & Verwaltungs GmbH, Haren, appointed as managing owners. 1986 sold to Ilmensee

15) HELGA WEHR (3)

Shipping Co. Ltd., Limassol (CYP), NORA still managing owners. 1986 renamed CINDY. 1989 sold to Caroline Shipping Co. Ltd., St. John's (ATG), Oskar Wehr KG (GmbH & Co.) appointed as managing owners, renamed CAROLINE. September 1993 sold to Contor Maritim, Jork (CYP), renamed FJORD STAR. 1995 sold to Cymoon Shipping Co. Ltd., Limassol, mgrs. Medstar Shipmanagement Ltd., renamed OLIVIA, re-engined with an SBV9M628 engine (ex sunk fishtrawler) with 1745 kW, made by Klöckner-Humboldt-Deutz, newly measured, now 1990 GT/3050 tdw. 2001 still trading.

17) CHRISTINA

17) Singledeck motorship CHRISTINA

1599 GRT / 3050 tw – 80.68 x 14.33 x 5.11 m – 1 four-stroke six-cylinder MWM engine, 2205 kW

6.5.1977 launched. August 1977 completed by Scheepswerf 'Waterhuizen' NV J. Pattje, Waterhuizen (No. 331) as SUSANNA for BV Equator, Rotterdam (NLD). 1983 renamed GARDAZEE. 1986 sold to Noordlijn Holding BV, Delfzijl (NLD), NORA Reederei & Verwaltungs GmbH, Haren, appointed as managing owners. 1986 sold to Hubert Shipping Co. Ltd., Limassol (YP), NORA still managing owners, renamed HUBERT. 1979 sold to Christina Shipping Co. Ltd., St. John's (ATG), Oskar Wehr KG (GmbH & Co.) appointed as managing owners, renamed CHRISTINA.

15.6.1990 sank in River Weser at Bremen-Osterort after being in collision with Swedish tank motorship EK CLOUD. 26.6.1993 salvaged and towed into Bremer Vulkan dry dock for inspection, declared a constructive total loss. Sold to Rauman Romu OY, Finland for demolition. 1993 sold to Arcticsteel Ltd., Valletta (MLT), mgrs. Christina Shipping OY Ltd., Rauma, repaired, newly measured, now 1962 GT/3050 tdw, renamed SUSANNA. 1999 still in service.

18) Singledeck motorship SIGRID

V2QE – 1599 GRT / 3035 tdw – 80.68 x 14.33 x 6.33 m – 1 four-stroke six-cylinder MWM engine, 2205 kW

8.11.1977 launched. January 1978 completed by Scheepswerf 'Waterhuizen' NV J. Pattje, Waterhuizen (No. 333) as SILVIA for BV Equator, Delfzijl (NLD). 1982 sold to Scheepsbedrijf Noordlijn BV, Delfzijl. 1983 Intersee Schiffahrts GmbH, Haren, appointed as managing owners. 1983 renamed HELGAZEE. 1985 renamed HELGE. 1985 sold to Helgezee Shipping Co. Ltd., Limassol (CYP), NORA Reederei & Verwaltungs GmbH, Haren, appointed as managing owners. 1989 sold to Sigrid Shipping Co. Ltd., St. John's (ATG), Oskar Wehr KG (GmbH & Co.) appointed as managing owners. 1993 sold to Star Aries Shipmanagement Ltd., Limassol, renamed GOLF STAR. 1994 sold to Golf Star Shipping Ltd., Limassol, mgrs. unchanged. 20.10.1995 went aground on Scalpay in a position 57.51 N / 06.41

18) SIGRID

W during a voyage from Arklow to Rostock and was abandoned by her crew the following day. Later on the vessel was broken into parts by bad weather.

19) HUMBER STAR ex BIRTE WEHR

19) Tweendeck motorship BIRTE WEHR / HUMBER STAR

DGLK / V2MG – *999 GRT / 1939 GT / 2886 tdw / 90 TEU – 87.95 x 11.30 x 6.75 m – 1 four-stroke eight-cylinder Klöckner-Humboldt-Deutz engine, 735 kW*

December 1982 launched. 11.12.1982 completed by J. J. Sietas Schiffswerft, Neuenfelde (No. 920) as KATJA for Jürgen Stahmer KG, Hamburg (DEU). 7.7.1987 until 9.5.1989 flagged out to Antigua and Barbuda (ATG). 31.5.1990 sold to Partenreederei, Hamburg, Oskar Wehr KG (GmbH & Co.) appointed as managing owners, renamed BIRTE WEHR. 12.1.1993 flagged out to Antigua and Barbuda (ATG), mgrs. now Star Aries Shipmanagement Ltd. 1994 mgrs. Contor Mairitim Klaus Vorwerk. 1994 renamed HUMBER STAR, Funafuti (TUV), mgrs. Oskar Wehr KG (GmbH & Co.). 1994 transferred to Star Ionian Shipping Co. Ltd., mgrs. Star Aries Shipmanagement Ltd., newly measured, now 1939 GT/2886 tdw. 1999 renamed BIRTE WEHR. 1999 sold to Partenreederei MS 'Dixi', Limassol (CYP), Mgrs. L & L Shipping Ltd., renamed NANDIA. 2001 still trading.

20) Containership IMKE WEHR / IBN KHALDOUN

V2SC – *6819 GT / 7676 tdw / 518 TEU – 122.10 x 20.10 x 10.90 – one four-stroke 12-cylinder engine with 4413 kW, built by VEB Maschinenbau Halberstadt*

14.10.1985 launched. 20.12.1985 completed by S. A. Juliana Constructora Gijonesa, Gijon (No. 305) as JOHANNGEORGENSTADT for VEB Deutfracht/Seereederei, Rostock (EG). 18.6.1990 transferred to Deutsche Seereederei Rostock GmbH, Rostock (DEU). July 1992 sold to Marsfjord Shipping Co. Ltd., Limassol (CYP). July 1992 sold to Imke Wehr Shipping Co. Ltd., St. John's (ATG), Oskar Wehr KG (GmbH & Co.), Hamburg, appointed as managing owners, renamed IMKE WEHR. 1992 renamed IBN KHALDOUN. 1993 renamed IMKE WEHR. 1996 renamed TIGER CREEK. October 1996 sold to Menkar Gemiçilik AS, Izmir (TUR), renamed VIVIEN A. 2001 still trading.

20) IMKE WEHR

21) Containership KHYBER / PETER WEHR

V2SI – *6819 GT / 7676 tdw / 518 TEU – 122.10 x 20.10 x 10.90 m – one four-stroke 12-cylinder engine with 4413 kW, built by VEB Maschinenbau Halberstadt*

October 1985 launched. 16.4.1986 completed by S. A. Juliana Constructora Gijonesa, Gijon

21) PETER WEHR

(No. 305) as JÖHSTADT for VEB Deutfracht/Seereederei, Rostock (EG). 18.6.1990 transferred to Deutsche Seereederei Rostock GmbH, Rostock (DEU). July 1992 sold to Marsfjord Shipping Co. Ltd., Limassol (CYP). July 1992 sold to Peter Wehr Shipping Co. Ltd., St. John's (At), Oskar Wehr KG (GmbH & Co.) appointed as managing owners, renamed KHYBER. 1993 renamed PETER WEHR. 1994 renamed SAMUDERA THAI. 1995 renamed PETER WEHR. 1995 renamed FMG AMERICA. 1996 renamed PETER WEHR. 1996 sold to Mizar Gemiçilik AS, Istanbul (TUR), renamed WANDA A. 2001 still trading.

22) **Containership**

22.525 tdw / 1618 TEU – 168.00 x 27.00 m – two-stroke seven-cylinder Sulzer engine, 21 knots
Ordered in June 1993 from MTW Schiffswerft GmbH (No. 293) for delivery November 1994, intended name WEHR OAKLAND. Later sold to Reederei Hermann Buss GmbH & Cie., Leer. 25.10.1994 completed as ELBE TRADER.

23) **Containership**

22.525 tdw / 1618 TEU – 168.00 x 27.00 m – 1 two-stroke seven-cylinder Sulzer engine, 21 knots
Ordered in June 1993 from MTW Schiffswerft GmbH (No. 294) for delivery November 1994, intended name WEHR SYDNEY. Later sold to Reederei Hermann Buss GmbH & Cie., Leer. 20.9.1994 launched. In January 1995 completed as TRAVE TRADER.

24) **Container motorship**
SIGRID WEHR (2) / INDEPENDENT VENTURE / WASHINGTON EXPRESS

ELSU5 – *10,917 GT / 13,700 tdw / 1170 TEU – 151.00 x 24.00 x 11.10/8.25 m – 1 four-stroke seven-cylinder engine with 9730 kW, made by MAN, 18.5 knots*

22.11.1995 launched as CAPE SCOTT for Columbia Shipmanagement Ltd., Limassol (CYP). Prior to completion sold to MS. 'Sigrid Wehr' Schiffahrtsges. mbH & Co., Monrovia (LBR), mgrs. Oskar Wehr KG (GmbH & Co.), Hamburg, renamed SIGRID WEHR. 29.12.1995 completed by Stocznia Szczecinska, Szczecin (No. B 190-I/2) and delivered. Early 1996 renamed INDEPENDENT VENTURE. 1997 renamed SIGRID WEHR. In April 1997 fitted with two 40-tonne cranes. 2000 renamed WASHINGTON EXPRESS. 2001 still trading.

24) SIGRID WEHR

25) **Container motorship**
WEHR ALTONA / CSAV RIO DE LA PLATA / KOTA SEJARAH / CSAV NINGBO / NORASIA YANTIAN / LYKES PATHFINDER

DGYR – *16,801 GT / 22,900 tdw / 1730 TEU - 176.36 x 25.30 x 13.50 / 9.90 m – 1 two-stroke six-cylinder engine with 13,320 kW, built by H. Cegielski, Poznan, under licence by Gebr. Sulzer, 20 knots*

25) CSAV RIO DE LA PLATA

Launched as WEHR ALTONA. 22.9.1997 completed by Stocznia Szczecinska SA, Szczecin (No. B 170-I/9) completed as CSAV RIO DE LA PLATA for DS Rendite Fonds Nr. 60 MS 'Wehr Altona' GmbH & Co. Containerschiff KG, Dortmund/Hamburg (DEU), KR Oskar Wehr KG (GmbH & Co.). 1999 renamed KOTA SEJARAH. 2000 renamed CSAV NINGBO. 2000 renamed NORASIA YANTIAN. 2001 renamed LYKES PATHFINDER. 2001 still trading.

26) INDAMEX NHAVA SHEVA

26) **Container motorship**
WEHR OTTENSEN / CSAV RIO GRANDE / INDAMEX NHAVA SHEVA
DGWM – *16,801 GT / 22,900 tdw / 1730 TEU- 176.36 x 25.30 x 13.50 / 9.90 m – 1 two-stroke six-cylinder engine with 13,320 kW, built by H. Cegielski, Poznan, under licence by Gebr. Sulzer, 20 knots*
Launched as WEHR OTTENSEN. 2.10.1997 completed by Stocznia Szczecinska SA, Szczecin (No. B 170-I/10) as CSAV RIO GRANDE for MS 'Wehr Ottensen' Schiffahrtsges. mbH & Co., Hamburg (DEU), KR Oskar Wehr KG (GmbH & Co.). 2000 renamed WEHR OTTENSEN. 2001 renamed INDAMEX NHAVA SHEVA. 2001 still trading.

27) CSAV RIO AMAZONAS

27) **Container motorship**
WEHR KOBLENZ / CSAV RIO AMAZONAS / PANAMERICAN / DGWH – *16,801 GT / 22,900 tdw / 1730 TEU – 176.36 x 25.30 x 13.50 / 9.90 m – 1 two-stroke six-cylinder engine with 13,320 kW, built by H. Cegielski, Poznan, under licence by Gebr. Sulzer, 20 knots*
Launched as WEHR KOBLENZ. 11.2.1998 completed by Stocznia Szczecinska SA, Szczecin (No. B 170-I/11) as CSAV RIO AMAZONAS for MS 'Wehr Koblenz' Schiffahrtsges. mbH & Co., Hamburg (DEU), KR Oskar Wehr KG (GmbH & Co.). 1999 renamed PANAMERICAN. 2001 still trading.

28) WEHR MÜDEN

28) Container motorship CSAV RIMAC / WEHR MÜDEN / CROWLEY EXPRESS / CSAV VALENCIA / TMM QUETZAL

DAZG – 16,801 GT / 23,040 tdw / 1730 TEU – 176.36 x 25.30 x 13.50 / 9.90 m – 1 two-stroke six-cylinder engine with 13,320 kW, built by H. Cegielski, Poznan, under licence by Gebr. Sulzer, 20 knots

20.12.1997 launched as WEHR MÜDEN. 26.3.1998 completed by Stocznia Szczecinska SA, Szczecin (Bau-Nr. B 170-I/12) as CSAV RIMAC for DS-Rendite Fonds Nr. 63 MS Wehr Mosel GmbH & Co. Containerschiff KG (DEU) KR Oskar Wehr KG (GmbH & Co.) In January 1999 renamed CROWLEY EXPRESS. May 2000 renamed CSAV VALENCIA. July 2000 renamed WEHR MÜDEN. 2001 renamed TMM QUETZAL. 2001 still trading.

30) WEHR RISSEN

29) WEHR FLOTTBEK

29) Container motorship WEHR FLOTTBEK / ALIANCA BAHIA

ELXB4 – 16,801 GT / 23,040 tdw / 1730 TEU – 176.36 x 25.30 x 13.50 / 9.90 m – 1 two-stroke six-cylinder engine with 13,320 kW, built by H. Cegielski, Poznan, under licence by Gebr. Sulzer, 20 knots

10.4.1999 launched. End June 1999 completed by Stocznia Szczecinska SA, Szczecin (No. B 170-III/12) as WEHR FLOTTBEK for MS 'Wehr Flottbek' Schiffahrtsges. mbH & Co. KG, Hamburg, KR Oskar Wehr KG (GmbH & Co.), Hamburg. 2000 renamed ALIANCA BAHIA. 2001 still trading.

30) Container motorship WEHR RISSEN / CMA-CGM BOUGAINVILLE

ELXB3 – 16,801 GT / 23,040 tdw / 1730 TEU – 176.36 x 25.30 x 13.50 / 9.90 m – 1 two stroke six- cylinder engine with 13,320 kW, built by H. Cegielski, Poznan, under licence by Gebr. Sulzer, 20 knots

5.5.1999 launched. Mid July 1999 completed by Stocznia Szczecinska SA, Szczecin (No. B 170-III/13) as WEHR RISSEN for MS 'Wehr Rissen' Schiffahrtsges. mbh & Co. KG, Monrovia (LBR), KR Reederei Oskar Wehr KG (GmbH & Co.), Hamburg. 2000 renamed CMA-CGM BOUGAINVILLE. 2001 still trading.

31) HUGO SELMER (2)

31) Motor bulkcarrier HUGO SELMER (2)

V7CM4 – 39,537 GT / 65,427 tdw – 254.10 x 32.20 x 17.00 / 12.35 m – 1 two-stroke six-cylinder engine with 12,799 kW, built by UCM Resta, Resita, under licence of MAN

1986 completed by Santierul Naval 2 Mai Mangalia, Mangalia (No. 900/154) as BORCEA for Interprinderea de Explotare a Floti Maritima NAVROM, Constanta (ROM). 1991 sold to Neptune Hope Maritime Ltd., Valletta (MLT), Mgrs. Ermis Maritime Corporation, Piraeus, renamed TOMIS HOPE. In May 1999 sold to SBT Star Bulk & Tankers (Germany) GmbH & Co. KG, Hamburg (MLT),KR Reederei Oskar Wehr KG (GmbH & Co.), renamed HUGO SELMER. 2000 transferred under Marshall Islands flag (MHL), homeport Majuro. 2001 still trading.

33) MIMI SELMER

33) **Motor bulkcarrier MIMI SELMER**

V7CM5 – *39,537 GT / 65,427 tdw – 254.10 x 32.20 x 17.00 / 12.87 m – 1 two-stroke six-cylinder engine with 12,799 kW, built by UCM Resita, Resita, under licence of MAN*

1987 completed by Santierul Naval 2 Mai Mangalia, Mangalia (No. 900/155) as BANISOR for Interprinderea de Explotare a Floti Maritima NAVROM, Constanta (ROM). 1991 sold to Neptune Hope Maritime Ltd., Valletta (MLT), Mgrs. Ermis Maritime Corporation, Piraeus, renamed TOMIS FAITH. 11.5. 1999 at Gdynia taken over by SBT Star Bulk & Tankers (Germany) GmbH & Co. KG, Hamburg (MLT), KR Reederei Oskar Wehr KG (GmbH & Co.), renamed MIMI SELMER. 2000 transferred under Marshall Islands flag (MHL), homeport Majuro. 2001 still trading.

32) FREDERIKE SELMER

32) **Motor bulkcarrier FREDERIKE SELMER**

V7CM6 – *39,537 GT / 65,427 tdw – 253.98 x 32.21 x 17.00 / 12.35 m – 1 two-stroke six-cylinder engine with 12,799 kW, built by UCM Resita, Resita, under licence of MAN*

1985 completed by Santierul Naval 2 Mai Mangalia, Mangalia (No. 900/152) as BASARABI for Interprinderea de Explotare a Floti Maritima NAVROM, Constanta (ROM). 1991 sold to Neptune Glory Maritime Ltd., Valletta (MLT), Mgrs. Ermis Maritime Corporation, Piraeus, renamed TOMIS GLORY. 11.5.1999 in Hamburg taken over by SBT Star Bulk & Tankers (Germany) GmbH & Co. KG, Hamburg (MLT), KR Reederei Oskar Wehr KG (GmbH & Co.), renamed FREDERIKE SELMER. 2000 transferred under Marshall Islands flag (MHL), homeport Majuro. 2001 still trading.

34) THOMAS SELMER

34) **Motor bulkcarrier THOMAS SELMER**
V7CM7 *– 39,537 GT / 65,427 tdw – 254.10 x 32.20 x 17.00 / 12.35 m – 1 two-stroke six-cylinder engine with 12,799 kW, built by UCM Resta, Resita, under licence of MAN*
1985 completed by Santierul Naval 2 Mai Mangalia, Mangalia (No. 900/153) as BARAOLT for Interprinderea de Explotare a Floti Maritima NAVROM, Constanta (ROM). 1991 sold to Neptune Hope Maritime Ltd., Valletta (MLT), Mgrs. Ermis Maritime Corporation, Piraeus, renamed TOMIS SPIRIT. 11.5.1999 in Hamburg taken over by SBT Star Bulk & Tankers (Germany) GmbH & Co. KG, Hamburg (MLT), KR Reederei Oskar Wehr KG (GmbH & Co.), renamed THOMAS SELMER. 2000 transferred under Marshall Islands flag (MHL), homeport Majuro. 2001 still trading.

35) **Motor containership ILLAPEL / NORASIA MONTREAL (WEHR BLANKENESE)**
V7CL3 *– 16,177 GT / 23,021 tdw / 1730 TEU – 184.10 x 25.30 x 15.90 / 9.90 m – 1 two-stroke six-cylinder engine with 13,320 kW, made by H. Cegielski, Poznan, under licence of Sulzer, 20 knots*
21.9.1999 launched. 14.12.1999 completed by Stocznia Szczecinska SA, Szczecin (No. B 170-I/20) as ILLAPEL for Malleco Shipping Co. SA., Nassau (BHS), Mgrs. Compania Sud Americana de Vapores SA, Valparaiso. 27. May 2000 at San Antonio (Chile) handed over to Wehr Containerships GmbH & Co. KG, Majuro (MHL), KR Reederei Oskar Wehr KG (GmbH & Co.), Hamburg. 2000 renamed NORASIA MONTREAL. 26.6.2000 sold to MS Wehr Blankenese Schiffahrtsgesellschaft mbH & Co. KG, Hamburg. 2001 still trading.

35) ILLAPEL

36) **Motor containership ELQUI (WEHR SCHULAU)**
V7CL4 *– 16,177 GT / 23,026 tdw / 1730 TEU – 184.10 x 25.30 x 15.90 / 9.90 m – 1 two-stroke six-cylinder engine with 13,320 kW, made by H. Cegielski, Poznan, under licence of Sulzer, 20 knots*
28.8.1999 launched. 20.11.1999 completed by Stocznia Szczecinska SA, Szczecin (No. B 170-I/19) as ELQUI for Maule Shipping Co. SA., Nassau (BHS), Mgrs. Compania Sud Americana de Vapores SA, Valparaiso. 22.5.2000 in Brasil handed over to Wehr Containerships GmbH & Co. KG, Majuro (MHL), KR Reederei Oskar Wehr KG (GmbH & Co.), Hamburg. 27.11.2000 sold to MS Wehr Schulau Schiffahrtsgesellschaft mbH & Co. KG, Hamburg. 2001 still trading.

37) **Motor containership Newbuilding WEHR NIENSTEDTEN**
16,177 GT / 23,021 tdw / 1730 TEU – 184.10 x 25.30 x 15.90 / 9.90 m – 1 two-stroke six-cylinder engine with 13,320 kW, made by H. Cegielski, Poznan, under licence of Sulzer, 20 knots
In May 2000 ordered from Stocznia Szczecinska SA, Szczecin (No. B 170-III/16) for delivery fourth quarter 2001.

38) **Motor containership Newbuilding WEHR FALKENSTEIN**
16,177 GT / 23,021 tdw / 1730 TEU – 184.10 x 25.30 x 15.90 / 9.90 m – 1 two-stroke six-cylinder engine with 13,320 kW, made by H. Cegielski, Poznan, under licence of Sulzer, 20 knots
In May 2000 ordered from Stocznia Szczecinska SA, Szczecin (No. B 170-III/17) for delivery fourth quarter 2001.

39) **Motor containership**
   Newbuilding WEHR ELBE
25,600 GT / 33,600 tdw / 2524 TEU – 208.16 x 29.80 x 16.40 / 10.10 m – 1 two-stroke engine with 19,800 kW
In June 2000 ordered from Kvaerner Warnow Werft GmbH, Warnemünde (No. 24) for delivery fourth quarter 2001.

40) **Motor containership**
   Newbuilding WEHR WESER
25,600 GT / 33,600 tdw / 2524 TEU – 208.16 x 29.80 x 16.40 / 10.10 m – 1 two-stroke engine with 19,800 kW
In June 2000 ordered from Kvaerner Warnow Werft GmbH, Warnemünde (No. 25) for delivery fourth quarter 2001.

41) **Motor containership**
   Newbuilding WEHR ALSTER
25,500 GT / 33,750 tdw / 2524 TEU / 19,810 kW
12.4.2000 orderd by E. R. Schiffahrt GmbH & Cie., Hamburg, from Volkswerft Stralsund (No. 438) for delivery in May 2002. Contract taken over by Reederei Oskar Wehr KG (GmbH & Co.) 30.6.2000.

42) **Motor containership**
   Newbuilding WEHR BILLE
25,500 GT / 33,750 tdw / 2524 TEU / 19,810 kW
12.4.2000 orderd by E. R. Schiffahrt GmbH & Cie., Hamburg, from Volkswerft Stralsund (No. 439) for delivery in July 2002. Contract taken over by Reederei Oskar Wehr KG (GmbH & Co.) 30.6.2000.

43) **Motor containership**
   Newbuilding WEHR TRAVE
25,600 GT / 33,600 tdw / 2524 TEU – 208.16 x 29.80 x 16.40 / 10.10 m – 1 two-stroke engine with 19,800 kW
In December 2000 ordered from Kvaerner Warnow Werft GmbH, Warnemünde (No. 26) for delivery in March 2002.

44) **Motor containership**
   Newbuilding WEHR WARNOW
25,600 GT / 33,600 tdw / 2524 TEU – 208.16 x 29.80 x 16.40 / 10.10 m – 1 two-stroke engine with 19,800 kW
In December 2000 ordered from Kvaerner Warnow Werft GmbH, Warnemünde (No. 27) for delivery in May 2002.

45) **Motor containership**
   Newbuilding WEHR TBN 1
25,600 GT / 33,600 tdw / 2524 TEU – 208.16 x 29.80 x 16.40 / 10.10 m – 1 two-stroke engine with 19,800 kW
In December 2000 ordered from Kvaerner Warnow Werft GmbH, Warnemünde (No. 28) for delivery in September 2002.

46) **Motor containership**
   Newbuilding WEHR TBN 2
25,600 GT / 33,600 tdw / 2524 TEU – 208.16 x 29.80 x 16.40 / 10.10 m – 1 two-stroke engine with 19,800 kW
In December 2000 ordered from Kvaerner Warnow Werft GmbH, Warnemünde (No. 29) for delivery in November 2002.

37) ELQUI

Vessels In Service

Vessels Name	Charter Name	Type	Built	Dead-weight	Gross Tonnage	Capacity	Flag
Thomas Wehr		Ro/Ro	1977	4000 tdw	7635 GT	91 Trailer	Tuvalu
Gabriele Wehr		Ro/Ro	1978	4000 tdw	7635 GT	91 Trailer	Tuvalu
Sigrid Wehr		Container	1996	13700 tdw	10917 GT	1150 TEU	Liberia
Wehr Altona		Container	1997	23040 tdw	16801 GT	1730 TEU	Germany
Wehr Ottensen		Container	1997	23051 tdw	16801 GT	1730 TEU	Germany
Wehr Koblenz		Container	1998	23026 tdw	16801 GT	1730 TEU	Germany
Wehr Müden		Container	1998	23029 tdw	16801 GT	1730 TEU	Germany
Wehr Flottbek		Container	1999	23000 tdw	16801 GT	1730 TEU	Liberia
Wehr Rissen		Container	1999	23000 tdw	16801 GT	1730 TEU	Liberia
Wehr Blankenese		Container	1999	23000 tdw	16801 GT	1730 TEU	Marshall Islands
Wehr Schulau		Container	1999	23000 tdw	16801 GT	1730 TEU	Marshall Islands
Hugo Selmer		Bulk	1986	65427 tdw	39537 GT	92016 cbm	Marshall Islands
Mimi Selmer		Bulk	1987	65360 tdw	39537 GT	92016 cbm	Marshall Islands
Thomas Selmer		Bulk	1985	65982 tdw	39537 GT	92016 cbm	Marshall Islands
Frederike Selmer		Bulk	1986	65275 tdw	39539 GT	92016 cbm	Marshall Islands

Vessels On Order

Vessels Name	Hull No.	Type	Delivery	Dead-weight	Gross Tonnage	Capacity	Shipyard
Wehr Nienstedten	B170-III/16	Container	Oct. 2001	23000 tdw	16801 GT	1730 TEU	Stocznia Szczecinska S.A Szczecin, Poland
Wehr Falkenstein	B170-III/17	Container	Dec. 2001	23000 tdw	16801 GT	1730 TEU	Stocznia Szczecinska S.A Szczecin, Poland
Wehr Elbe	CV 2500 Hull 024	Container	Oct. 2001	33600 tdw	25600 GT	2524 TEU	Kvaerner Warnow Werft Warnemünde, Germany
Wehr Weser	CV 2500 Hull 025	Container	Nov. 2001	33600 tdw	25600 GT	2524 TEU	Kvaerner Warnow Werft Warnemünde, Germany
Wehr Trave	CV 2500 Hull 026	Container	Mar. 2002	33600 tdw	25600 GT	2524 TEU	Kvaerner Warnow Werft Warnemünde, Germany
Wehr Warnow	CV 2500 Hull 027	Container	May 2002	33600 tdw	25600 GT	2524 TEU	Kvaerner Warnow Werft Warnemünde, Germany
Wehr Alster	VW 2500.1 Hull 438	Container	May 2002	33750 tdw	25500 GT	2524 TEU	Volkswerft Stralsund Stralsund, Germany
Wehr Bille	VW 2500.1 Hull 439	Container	Jul. 2002	33750 tdw	25500 GT	2524 TEU	Volkswerft Stralsund Stralsund, Germany
Wehr TBN 1	CV 2500 Hull 028	Container	Sep. 2002	33600 tdw	25600 GT	2524 TEU	Kvaerner Warnow Werft Warnemünde, Germany
Wehr TBN 2	CV 2500 Hull 029	Container	Nov. 2002	33600 tdw	25600 GT	2524 TEU	Kvaerner Warnow Werft Warnemünde, Germany

June 2001

Register (fett gedruckte Seitenzahlen weisen auf Abbildungen hin)

ADELIA TRICOLI 130
AEGIR **22,** 23
ALIANCA BAHIA 139
ALTAPPEN 134
ANDROMACHE I 129
ANKARA 26
ANNE (Selmer) 33
ANNE 37, **39,** 49, 44, 45, 46 , **47,** 48, 49, 50, 51, **121, 128**
ASIAN SENATOR 134

BALDER EEMS 115
BANISOR 140
BARAOLT 141
BASARABI 140
BERTHA KIENASS 44
BILLY 131
BIRTE WEHR 8, 100, 102 **123, 136**
BISMARCK 30, 31
BLUE MARLIN 131
BORCEA 140
BRIGITTE RAABE 13, 21

CAPE SCOTT 137
CAPITAINE LE BASTARD 24
CAROL S 131
CAROLINE 98, **123, 134**
CHRISTINA 98, 99, **123, 135**
CINDY 135
CITY OF AMSTERDAM 134
CMA-CGM BOUGAINVILLE 139
CMB ENERGY **97,** 134
CONTAINERSHIPS I 94
CONTI HOLANDIA 131
CROWLEY EXPRESS 139
CSAV NINGBO 137, 138

CSAV RIMAC 108, **109**
CSAV RIO AMAZONAS 108, **138**
CSAV RIO DE LA PLATA **107,** 137, **138**
CSAV RIO GRANDE 107, **138**
CSAV VELENCIA 139

DANA GERMANIA 133
DÖRTE **53, 128**
DORATHEA 8, 9, 16, 21
DUVENSTEDT 129

EK CLOUD 99, 135
ELBE I 128
ELBE TRADER 137
ELQUI 115, 141, **142**
EMDEN 43
EUROPA 78

FAIRLIGHT 133
FALLSUND 74, 131
FJORD STAR 135
FLEETWING 74, 131
FMG AMERICA 137
FREDERIKE SELMER 115, **126, 140**
FULDATAL 133

GABRIELE W 129,
GABRIELE WEHR (1) 65, **67, 121,** 129, **130**
GABRIELE WEHR (2) 70, 81, **85, 86**, 88, **90/91,** 92, 95, 96, **123**
GERORO 133
GLÜCKAUF 32
GOLF STAR **135**

HARTFORD EXPRESS (1) 78, 79, **80, 122, 131**

HARTFORD EXPRESS (2) 134
HEINZ SUHR 129
HELENA HUSMANN 88
HELGA WEHR (1) **52**, 53, 54, 56, 59, 60, 61, 62, **63,** 66, **121,** 128
HELGA WEHR (2) **5,** 65, **68,** 69, 70, 81, **121, 130**
HELGA WEHR (3) 96, 97, **100,** 103, **123**
HOHENBUCHEN 62, 128
HORNLINK 133
HUBERT 135
HUGO SELMER (1) **74,** 78, **122, 130**
HUGO SELMER (2) 115, **126, 139,** 140
HUMBER STAR 136

IBN KHALDOUN 136
ILLAPEL 116, 117, **141**
ILSE H 67, 128
INDEPENDENT VENTURE 105, **106,** 137
IMKE WEHR **101,** 102, **123, 136**

JANNE WEHR (1) 76, **77,** 78, **79, 122, 131**
JANNE WEHR (2) 69, 81, **83,** 94, 96, **122, 123, 132**
JÖHSTADT 102, 137
JOHANNGEORGENSTADT 102, 136
JÜRGEN W 131, **132**
JÜRGEN WEHR (1) **57,** 58, 60, 62, 69, 71, 78, **121**

KADUNA 134
KÄTE 21
KAIRO 117
KATJA 135
KEHRWIEDER 9
KHYBER 102, 136, 137
KOTA SEJARAH **107, 137,** 138

LUDWIG SANDERS 53, 128

MAERSK BELLA 134
MAERSK CLAUDINE **97**, 134
MANA 133
MAR DEL PLATA 27, 28, 29, 43
MARGARETHA NIBBE 21, **22**
MARIANNE WEHR 62, **63,** 64, 65, 78, **121, 129**
MICHEL 93
MIMI SELMER (Selmer) 32, **33,** 34, **35**
MIMI SELMER **115, 126, 140**
MINA 131
MODAG 34

NANDIA 135
NAVEN 54
NORASIA MONTREAL 141
NORASIA YANTIAN 137
NORDSEE 31

OLIVIA 135
OUTER GABBARD 60

P & O NEDLLOYD CARACAS 134
PAMELA 93
PANAMERICAN 138
PETER WEHR (1) 78
PETER WEHR (2) **101,** 102, **123,** 136, **137**
PISHRO 134

QU JIANG 131

ROXANE KERSTEN 132

SAGITTA 82
SAMPO 24
SAMUDERA THAI 137
SANTA ANGELIKA 129

SANTA MARIA 133
SARI 133
SIGRID 98, **103, 123, 135**
SIGRID WEHR (1) 70, **87,** 88, 89, 92, 93, 96, 98, 123, **133**
SIGRID WEHR (2) 105, **106, 125, 137**
SOPHIE 15, 16, 18, 20
SPIRIT OFAMSTERDAM 134
STEFAN E 130
SUSANNA 135

THAMES STAR 132
THOMAS SELMER 115, **116, 126, 141**
THOMAS WEHR 84, 87, 88, 95, **123, 132, 133**
TIGER CREEK 136
TOMIS FAITH 115, 140
TOMIS GLORY 115, 140
TOMIS HOPE 115, 140
TOMIS SPIRIT 115, 141
TOR ANGLIA 95, 133
TOR NEERLANDIA 133
TRANSIT 93
TRAVE TRADER 137

UNITY I 131

VIGLA 131
VIRGINIA 131
VISCARIA 132
VIVIEN A 136

WACRO EXPRESS **85,** 132, 133
WANDA A. 137
WASSERSCHUTZPOLIZEI 15 40
WEHR ALSTER **126,** 142
WEHR ALTONA 107, **125,** 138
WEHR BILLE **126,** 142
WEHR BLANKENESE 115, 125
WEHR ELBE **126,** 142
WEHR FALKENSTEIN **125,** 141
WEHR FLOTTBEK 108, **109, 125,** 138, 139
WEHR KOBLENZ 108, **125**
WEHR MÜDEN 108, 109, **125,** 139
WEHR NIENSTEDTEN **125,** 141
WEHR OAKLAND 137
WEHR OTTENSEN 107, **125,** 138
WEHR RISSEN 108, **125, 139**
WEHR SCHULAU 115, **125**
WEHR SYDNEY 137
WEHR WESER **126**

Inhaltsverzeichnis

In Koblenz geboren, aber die Rheinschiffahrt lockte nicht	6
Auf kleinen Schiffen wurde viel gelernt	13
Mitkalkulieren der Frachtergebnisse schon am Anfang	20
Dampfer waren viel größer und komfortabler	23
Anstellung als Offizier und ein Entschluß	28
Die Familie Selmer von der Insel Sylt	30
Junge Ehe in schwierigen Zeiten	36
Finanzierung mit Fisch und Silberfüchsen	42
Einfallsreichtum bei zu kurzen Schleusen	49
Ein größeres Schiff mit scharfem Kiel	53
1957 lieferte Sietas den ersten Neubau	58
Mehr Urlaub für die Seeleute – mehr Schiffe	65
Der Kapitänsreeder und seine Kapitäne	69
Ein Schottland-Auftrag scheiterte an einem Ultimatum	73
Umzug vom Sofa in ein eigenes Büro	75
Das erste Schiff mit der optimalen Brücke	81
Diversifizierung mit neuen Schiffstypen	84
Ein spezielles Spezialschiff für Schwergut	88
Eine eigene Firma für die Befrachtung	92
Eine neue HELGA WEHR wurde Flaggschiff	96
Containerschiffsneubauten aus Polen	105
Ein schwerer Verlust für Familie und Reederei	110
Generations und Ortswechsel	111
Sprung in die Massengutfahrt und weitere Neubauten	115
Reeder Jürgen Wehr und seine langjährigen Mitarbeiter	118
Die Flotte	121
Die Schiffsliste	128
Register	145

Contents

The lure of the sea	6
An education on small ships	13
Calculations from the start	20
Steamships – bigger and more comfortable	23
Officer and Shipowner	28
The Selmer Family from Sylt	30
Young marriage – hard times	36
Fish and furs	42
Ingenuity in short locks	49
Larger ship – deeper keel	53
First ship from the Sietas yard	58
More shore leave – more ships	65
Owner-Master and his Captains	69
An ultimatum	73
The move to a proper office	75
The first ship with an ultra-modern bridge	81
Diversification – new types of ships	84
A special heavy lift carrier	88
A chartering company of its own	92
A new 'HELGA WEHR' – a new flag ship	96
New container ships from Poland	105
An acute loss for family and company	110
A new generation, new address	111
Additional bulk trade, more new shipbuilding	115
The ship owner, the shipping company	118
The Fleet	121
The List of Ships	128
Register	145